SACRED PLACES
IN NORTH AMERICA

SACRED

COURTNEY MILNE

PLACES IN NORTH AMERICA

A JOURNEY INTO THE MEDICINE WHEEL

STEWART, TABORI & CHANG

This book is dedicated
to the Spirit of White Buffalo Calf Woman,
who said one day when she returned to Earth,
the four peoples—red, yellow, black and white—would heal their
differences.

A female white buffalo calf named Miracle
was born on
August 20, 1994, near Janesville, Wisconsin

COURTNEY MILNE

Copyright © 1994, 1995 Courtney Milne
Originally published in 1994 by Penguin Books Canada Ltd.
in Canada under the title *Spirit of the Land*.

Published by Stewart, Tabori & Chang
A division of U.S. Media Holdings, Inc.
115 West 18th Street
New York, NY 10011

Designed by Nai Y. Chang

Library of Congress has cataloged the original edition as follows:

Milne, Courtney, 1943-
    Sacred Places in North America / Courtney Milne
        p.   cm.
    Includes bibliographical references (p. 124) and index.
    ISBN: 1-55670-414-3 (hbk.: alk paper) (Hardcover)
    ISBN: 1-55670-957-9 (Paperback)
    1. Indians of North America—Antiquities. 2. Sacred space—
    North America. 3. Medicine Wheel National Historic
    Landmark (Wyo.) 4. Indians of North America—Religion.
    5. Indian mythology—North America. 6. North America—
    Antiquities. I. Title
    E77.9.M54 1995
    299'.7—dc20   94-44794
        CIP

Printed in Singapore
10 9 8 7 6 5 4 3 2 1

Right: Gray Whales and dugout canoe, Grice Bay, Tofino,
Vancouver Island, British Columbia

Title Spread: Pictographs in unidentified cave, southern California

CONTENTS

ACKNOWLEDGMENTS

My first words of thanks go to Sherrill Miller, my mate and partner. Sherrill organized many of the trips and spearheaded the research and writing of the text.

Due to space limitations here, it is not possible to name the hundreds of people who have assisted us along the way. Special thanks to Nicole Price of the Medicine Wheel Alliance at Big Horn, Wyoming, for supporting me in my vision of this wheel as a means of providing direction for my journey around Great Turtle Island. I would like to express gratitude to the people of the Native American tribal offices throughout the United States and Canada who gave us permission to photograph and provided us with a treasure of leads on books and stories. Thank you also to the management and staff of the National Parks, Monuments and Forests in the United States, the National and Provincial Parks in Canada and the private parks represented in this book.

On the production side, thanks go to Danny Weselowski of Pro-Color Lab in Saskatoon for assistance with the computer manipulated composites; Randy Hills of Chromographics, Inc. in Saskatoon for making the slide sandwiches; and the staff of Gibson Photo in Saskatoon for their continued excellence in the processing of my slide film.

Special appreciation to Jackie Kaiser and the staff of Penguin Books, for assisting me in producing the Canadian edition, *Spirit of the Land, Sacred Places in Native North America,* upon which this book is based.

Finally, thanks to Nai Chang for the beautiful book design, editing and picture selection, and to Brian Maracle for a powerful and sensitive foreword.

FOREWORD

Our ancestors, the ancient ones, left many testaments to their existence. The signs of their being—serpent mounds, rock paintings, medicine wheels, petroglyphs, inukshuks, totem poles—have withstood the grinding pressure of time and are scattered all across Great Turtle Island.

The ancient works endure but the people who made them no longer exist. As their descendants we may have retained much of their language, culture and traditions but we are not the same people. Despite the passage of untold generations, however, the meaning of many of these works still lives within our hearts.

These monuments fuse us with our ancestral past. Because they help us to understand where we come from, they also help us to understand who we are. These works give meaning to our lives. They enrich our ceremonies, religions and cultures. They provide guidelines for behavior and inspiration for the future.

But the meaning of some of these monuments has been lost. Enveloped in mystery, they taunt us with frustratingly unanswerable questions: Who made it? How was it used? What does it mean?

People who have a strong link to the past do not mourn the loss of meaning from such creations. We simply accept that these works are the silent remnants of another people, another time.

But there is one thing about these ancient creations that should concern all of us—Aboriginal people and newcomers alike. At the core of each of these works is a statement that expresses the relationship that human beings have with each other, with the land and with their God. And it is clear from these markets of the past that the ancients of Great Turtle Island treated the land, each other and the Creator with reverence and respect.

The monuments the ancients left for us should therefore make us wonder: What will the monuments we leave for our descendants say about the way we treat each other? What will they say about the way we treat the land? And what will they say about our relationship with our Creator?

Clearly, it will be a long time before the humans on Great Turtle Island come to one mind about how to treat each other and how to relate to God. But if we are to leave monuments that awe and inspire future generations, then we will have to begin showing respect for one thing that most of the people here have come to take for granted—the land.

Great Turtle Island is scarred in many places because of greed and lack of respect. The forces of nature will help the land recover from the damage because the spirit of the land endures. It may not be the same, but the land will survive.

Few people today have the same relationship with the land that the original inhabitants did. Most of the people living here now are urban creatures, living in an environment they have shaped to their liking. Not only do they not live as part of the natural world, they rarely seek it out and avoid it whenever they can.

At best, most people regard "the land" as little more than an interesting subject for a television documentary. At worst, they regard it as a commodity—something to be shaped, tamed, exploited and controlled for profit and pleasure, for comfort and convenience.

To the Aboriginal people of Great Turtle Island, though, land is more than real estate and nature is more than an annoyance to heat or air-condition.

My people, the Iroquois—like probably all the other Aboriginal people—know from our teachings that we were created from the earth itself and specifically placed on this one corner of Great turtle Island by the Creator. Our very being stems from this one fact: we were born of this earth and to this earth.

Furthermore, the Creator gave our people, and our

people only, the knowledge of how to survive on this land, knowledge that we shared with those who came later. The Creator also gave us the instructions on how we should respect the land and how we should give thanks.

From all this, we believe in the deepest part of our soul that this land was divinely and expressly made for us by the hand of God.

It should come as no surprise, then, to learn that we regard the land—all of it—as sacred: every rock, every tree, every river, every blade of grass. All of creation—the four-legged, the swimming and the flying creatures, all of the plant life, the winds, the thunderers—everything from the most seemingly insignificant insect to the mightiest mountain is sacred, because it was made and placed here by the Creator.

And because all things are sacred, all places are sacred. The places we thank the Creator. The places the spirits live. The places we celebrate our ceremonies. The places we seek visions. The places we bury our dead. The places we name our children. The places we get our food. The places we gather our medicines. The places we greet the morning sun. The places we welcome the spring. The places we seek out for healing, contemplation and rejuvenation. All of the land on Great Turtle Island is hallowed ground because all of our activities are part of the sacred cycle of life.

One other thing must be understood: these sacred places are not nameless. They carry the names that we have given them in our ancestral language. These names give meaning to us and to our lives.

We shared these names with the newcomers just as we shared this land. We are now surrounded by the Aboriginal names of countless cities, rivers, lakes, parks, states and provinces—from Chicago and Chicoutimi to Wichita and Winnipeg. But after countless repetitions by people who don't know their meaning, these once-descriptive names have been stripped of their power, their magic and their beauty. Even the meaning of the country named Canada is known to just a few of the millions who call it home.

Five centuries after the newcomers arrived and began making their mark upon the land, we must ask ourselves: What kind of testaments are we leaving for our descendants?

Much of what we leave will last a thousand years, but there is little of which we can be proud. Most of the remnants of our being will testify to the lack of respect that the people now living on Great Turtle Island have for the land and the Creator.

But there are testaments being made of which we can be proud. Of those few, this book is one. This book is the kind of marker we should leave for the future—one that is wholeheartedly concerned with a relationship to the land and to the Creator, one that is based on reverence and respect.

There is much to be done if we are ever to create monuments for future generations which recapture the awe and wonder that are the hallmarks of the works of the ancient ones. We can start by learning the meaning of the Aboriginal ghost names that surround us, because the names of these places were divinely inspired. To learn and appreciate their true meaning will help to create much-needed respect for the land and the works of creation. We need to see the land for what it is—sacred in all its parts. And most of all, we need to develop and nurture a special relationship with the Creator that acknowledges the gifts of creation that have been bestowed upon us.

Akewenna'okon na' ne'e kenh iken. These are my words.

BRIAN MARACLE
SIX NATIONS GRAND RIVER TERRITORY, JANUARY 1994

INTRODUCTION

At the dawn of the 1990 autumn equinox, I climbed into the bucket of a hydraulic lift and was hoisted forty feet into the air beside the Big Horn Medicine Wheel in northern Wyoming. I felt a powerful energy there at the ten-thousand-foot summit of Medicine Mountain. It seemed to me that the Big Horn Wheel linked the distant plains with the heavens.

Though little is known for certain about its origins, the wheel is believed to be more than two thousand years old. The Crow, Arapaho and Shoshone peoples of this area all have oral histories about sacred ceremonies held here, and present-day prayer offerings can be found on a fence erected to protect the wheel. I did not know it at the time, but the Big Horn Wheel would figure prominently in my life in the coming years. The sense of mystery and awe I felt then has never left me.

In June, 1992, I participated in the Wisdom Keeper's Convocation, part of the non-governmental events at the Earth Summit in Rio de Janeiro, Brazil. While in Rio, I witnessed the signing of the Charter of the Indigenous People of the World, and was involved in lighting a ceremonial fire, a symbolic focus of spiritual energy from around the world. Soon after, I was presented with the idea of photographing sacred places in native North America. This immediately appealed to me because I have long felt a kinship with Native spiritual values.

I remembered my experience at Big Horn, and wondered where the twenty-eight spokes radiating from the central cairn might lead. A framework began to emerge. I decided to use the Big Horn Wheel as the starting point of my photographic journey, following each spoke across the continent in search of sacred landscapes.

The photographs in this book include specific sites that First Nations identify as holy, as well as other natural landforms that capture the mystical essence of the earth. Twenty years of photographing the land have drawn me ever closer to the life-giving cycles and rhythms of nature; I have long enjoyed discovering faces in tree bark and driftwood, and seeing animal or human figures in the land before me. The photographs in this book have been selected to convey my impressions of how it felt to be at these places. I have sometimes used special photographic techniques in an attempt to portray the spirit of the place—for me, small vignettes of nature are often more evocative than overall images of the physical landscape.

Today, despite centuries of oppression, this land's original inhabitants are finding new strength in their own traditions. The banning of such ceremonies as the Sundance, the Ghost Dance and the Potlatch, combined with the degradation of sacred lands through mining and development, are tragic events in the history of this continent. It is a testament to the enduring spiritual power of Native cultures that these traditions are now experiencing a resurgence.

For many North American Native people, the circle represents the cycle of life. On the circle, there is no beginning and no end. This symbol of infinity and interconnectedness is seen in the sweat lodge, the bowl of the sacred pipe, the sacred hoop and the medicine wheel. Some Native writers describe the medicine wheel as a microcosm of life, its circular pathway encompassing all aspects of the world within the four cardinal directions. Each of these directions represents a stage of life, within which specific lessons are learned. East is the place of birth and new beginnings; South, of youth, strength and idealism; West, of emotional growth and self-knowledge; and North, of wisdom and life's fulfillment. Corresponding to these directions are the four seasons—spring in the East, summer in the South, autumn in the West, and winter in the North—and the

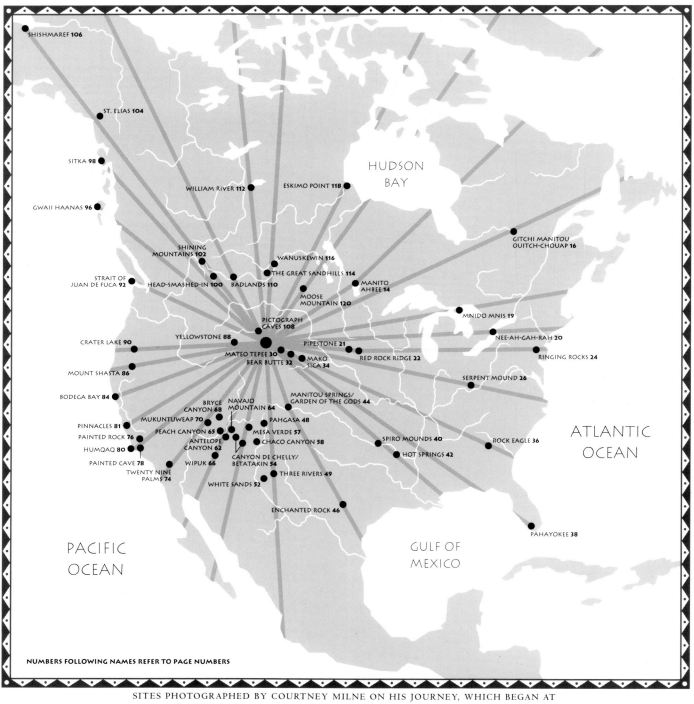

SHISHMAREF **106**

ST. ELÍAS **104**

SITKA **98**

GWAII HAANAS **96**

WILLIAM RIVER **112**

ESKIMO POINT **118**

HUDSON BAY

GITCHI MANITOU OUITCH-CHOUAP **16**

SHINING MOUNTAINS **102**

WANUSKEWIN **116**

THE GREAT SANDHILLS **114**

MANITO AHBEE **14**

STRAIT OF JUAN DE FUCA **92**

HEAD-SMASHED-IN **100**

BADLANDS **110**

MOOSE MOUNTAIN **120**

MNIDO MNIS **19**

NEE-AH-GAH-RAH **20**

PICTOGRAPH CAVES **108**

CRATER LAKE **90**

YELLOWSTONE **88**

PIPESTONE **21**

RED ROCK RIDGE **22**

RINGING ROCKS **24**

MATEO TEPEE **30**

BEAR BUTTE **32**

MAKO SICA **34**

MOUNT SHASTA **86**

SERPENT MOUND **26**

BODEGA BAY **84**

MANITOU SPRINGS/ GARDEN OF THE GODS **44**

BRYCE CANYON **68**

NAVAJO MOUNTAIN **64**

PINNACLES **81**

MUKUNTUWEAP **70**

PAHGASA **48**

SPIRO MOUNDS **40**

ROCK EAGLE **36**

ATLANTIC OCEAN

PAINTED ROCK **76**

PEACH CANYON **65**

MESA VERDE **57**

HUMQAQ **80**

ANTELOPE CANYON **62**

CHACO CANYON **58**

HOT SPRINGS **42**

PAINTED CAVE **78**

WIPUK **66**

CANYON DE CHELLY/ BETATAKIN **54**

TWENTY NINE PALMS **74**

THREE RIVERS **49**

WHITE SANDS **52**

ENCHANTED ROCK **46**

PACIFIC OCEAN

GULF OF MEXICO

PAHAYOKEE **38**

NUMBERS FOLLOWING NAMES REFER TO PAGE NUMBERS

SITES PHOTOGRAPHED BY COURTNEY MILNE ON HIS JOURNEY, WHICH BEGAN AT
THE BIG HORN MEDICINE WHEEL IN WYOMING

BIG HORN MEDICINE WHEEL, MEDICINE MOUNTAIN, WYOMING

elements of earth, wind, water and fire. The four related colors, according to the Lakota, are red, yellow, black and white, which also reflect the main races of the world. At Bear Butte, a hallowed mountain in South Dakota, the same four colors are seen in prayer flags tied to tree branches, and distinct soils of the same colors are found within a short walk of each other.

Although there are many similarities among Native spiritual traditions, there are also, of course, distinct variations. While it was impossible to address all of these within the scope of this book, it is important that these differences be respected, and to this end I have wherever possible, tried to include information about local traditions. Oral histories may vary, but the truth embodied in each telling endures.

This book is divided into four sections, each representing a cardinal direction. We begin our journey to the East of the Big Horn Medicine Wheel, visiting sites that fall in the paths leading to that section of the wheel, and continue to the South, West and North, so that the photographs of these time-honored places can be experienced within the context of the wheel that inspired the journey. My hope is that encountering these photographs will allow people to connect with the world as it was when all the land was revered, when all the elements were honored for their power, when wilderness provided spiritual as well as physical nourishment, and when all humankind respected the sacred nature of their surroundings. I think it is fitting to begin our journey with a prayer I found on a signpost at Bear Butte.

COURTNEY MILNE
GRANDORA, SASKATCHEWAN, JANUARY 1994

PRAYER TO THE FOUR WINDS

Great Spirit, I invoke the peace pipe in
reverence and gratitude of thy vast creation, of
which I am a part. To the life-giving of thy
servant, the sun and all heavenly bodies, the
blue sky, the great everlasting rocks, the
magnificent mountains with their fragrant
forests, pure streams and the animal kingdom.
We thank thee for all these gifts.

To the North and its guard, the White Eagle
Keep us pure and clean of mind,
Thoughts as white as thy blanket, the snow.
Make us hardy.

To the East and thy sentry, the Red Eagle
Grant us light that we may see our faults
And have better understanding with everyone.

To the South, and thy sentinel, Brown Eagle
The beautiful one, grant us warmth of heart,
Love and kindness to all.

To the West and the Thunder Bird
Who flies over the universe hidden in a cloak of
Rain clouds and cleanses the world of filth,
Cleanse our bodies and souls of all evil things.

To Mother Earth we come from thee and will
   return to thee,
Keep us in plenty that our days may be long
   with thee,

Great Spirit we thank thee and appreciate all
   these wonderful gifts to us.
Have pity on us.

EAST

To the East and thy sentry, the Red Eagle / Grant us light that we may see our faults / And have better understanding with everyone.

MANITO AHBEE • PLACE OF BEGINNING

THE STORY OF THE ORIGIN OF MAN

Here at Manito Ahbee, it is said the Original Man was lowered by rope from the sky to become the first inhabitant of Turtle Island, so named because after the Great Flood, the Earth was formed on the back of a turtle. It is here that Original Man received from the Great Spirit the following seven sacred teachings: wisdom, love, respect, bravery, honesty, humility and truth—the principles to guide the Anishanabe in caring for the earth and for each other. These teachings have been recorded in the stone shapes of animal figures and geometric designs called petroforms, which are unique to Manito Ahbee.

The age of the petroforms is not known, but the Anishanabe believe they were built by spirits as a physical reminder of their sacred instructions. One form of a turtle and snake is said to interpret the afterlife journey of the spirit. Some are used ceremonially by medicine people during tobacco offerings and healing rituals. At Bannock Point, one of two major sites in the area of Manito Ahbee, a human effigy lies face up, arms and legs outstretched. According to the Medewewin, an Anishanabe asked Waynaboozhoo (also known as Nanabush, or in Cree as Wesake Jack) to grant him everlasting life. Waynaboozhoo, who was both spirit and man, both trickster and guide, complied by turning him forever into a stone effigy.

Today Manito Ahbee is revered by the Anishanabe as a gateway to higher understanding, as a site of origin that is connected to other spiritual centers on our planet. It will stand for eternity as a place to teach, to heal and to pray.

COMPOSITE OF MOON, TREES AND HUMAN EFFIGY, BANNOCK POINT PETROFORM SITE, MANITOBA

This site is revered as a teaching and healing place by the Three Fires Confederacy, a society formed in the sixteenth century by the people who call themselves Anishanabe (meaning "Original People") from the Odawa, Potawatomi and Ojibway nations. Since the 1960s, a movement has been underway to revive the Three Fires Confederacy and its spiritual tradition, which is dedicated to the pursuit of sacred knowledge about the universe that will provide the Anishanabe with a spiritual balance. It is this Grand Medicine Society of Medewewin that has rekindled the creation story of the Anishanabe, who now number more than 250,000 throughout North America.

GITCHI MANITOU OUITCH-CHOUAP • HOUSE OF THE GREAT SPIRIT

CREE LEGEND

This remarkable cave, known as Gitchi Manitou Ouitch-chouap, or "House of the Great Spirit," has walls of smooth white marble that were polished by violent glacial streams. This was the place of protection and beauty where Cree hunters would come to pray to the Spirit of the Caribou or Moose for the gift of a good hunt. One Mistissini story says that the Memequash once resided here; these hairy-faced dwarfs lived in cliffs and paddled their stone canoes down the river to make rock paintings and to raid Indian fishnets.

FIRST SNOW ON LANDSCAPE, MISTISSINI, QUEBEC

MELTING SNOW ON WALL OF WHITE QUARTZITE CAVE, LA COLLINE BLANCHE, MISTISSINI, QUEBEC

La Colline Blanche is a huge outcropping of white quartzite along the southern shore of the Témiscamie River. To the local Mistissini Cree, this rock is known as Whapuushakanukw (pronounced wa-bush), meaning "House of the Rabbit." About 3,900 feet long and almost 1,500 feet high, it is mainly covered with trees except for a distinctly white talus slope high on the northwest side.

LEFT:
TOTEM LANDSCAPE, ROCKY
SHORELINE AND REFLECTION TURNED
90°, MANITOULIN ISLAND, ONTARIO

OPPOSITE:
PREDAWN LIGHT WITH RECEDING ICE ON
LAKE MANITOU, MANITOULIN ISLAND,
ONTARIO

BELOW:
ALDER BRANCH IN STREAM AT BRIDAL
VEIL FALLS, MANITOULIN ISLAND,
ONTARIO

Lake Mindemoya is where Nanabush, the trickster also known as Waynaboozhoo, stumbled as he was carrying his grandmother, and stopped to rub the magic alder bushes on his cuts and bruises. The alders turned red from his blood and remain that color to this day.

MNIDO MNIS • ISLAND OF THE GREAT SPIRIT

Manitoulin is the world's largest freshwater island, rising up between Lake Huron and Georgian Bay in Ontario. Based on translations from the Ojibway, Odawa (Ottawa) and Potawatomi languages, Manitou means "spirit," or "the Great Spirit." The island is also known as Gitchi Manitou, Manitoulin or Manitouminiss (Mnido Mnis), meaning "Isle of the Manitou" or "Spirit Island."

The story of Manitoulin's creation is rich in sacred significance. Gitchi Manitou had a dream, a vision of all that is good, and a mandate to fulfill his dream. He began by making the four elements—fire, earth, water and wind. From these he created the universe—the sun, moon, planets and the stars, bequeathing special powers to the land, the rivers, the lakes, the animals and the forest. He then created humans and bestowed on them the greatest gift of all—the ability to dream.

The Anishanabe Three Fires Confederacy decreed that all of Manitoulin is sacred, its spiritual stories recorded in the landscape. It is said that even today, Gitchi Manitou dwells on a tiny island in one of the large lakes on Manitoulin Island. Manitowaning Bay, known as "the den of the Great Spirit," is where Gitchi Manitou sometimes comes to travel through an underground secret passage in order to reach South Bay.

SNOW PUFFS ON BUSHES,
HORSESHOE FALLS,
NIAGARA FALLS, ONTARIO

Niagara Falls is by far the best-known cascade in North America, with five million visitors a year. The lure of this abyss is still strong; it is not uncommon to see daredevils driven by fame, and desperate people driven to suicide, challenging the fast-flowing waters over the falls.

NEE-AH-GAH-RAH • THUNDERING WATERS

IROQUOIS LEGEND

The Seneca and Huron call Niagara Falls Nee-ah-gah-rah, which means "Thundering Waters." Stories say the sound of the falls is the roar of the spirit living in the waters, who needed to be appeased every year with the sacrifice of a maiden in a canoe adorned with fruits and flowers.

In 1679, French explorers tried to stop Chief Eagle Eye from sacrificing his daughter Lela-wala. To ensure the ritual's completion, the chief and his daughter set out in separate canoes and both plunged to their deaths, then were transformed into spirits of strength and goodness that can still be felt today.

The Seneca and Huron also believe that the spirit of Lake Ontario is a serpent whose voice can be heard in the roar of the plunging waters, also known as "the place where thunder strikes." It is here that, according to Seneca legend, the Good Spirit who lives in the Cave of the Winds sent a thunderbolt to kill the serpent, causing the monster to thrash with such force that a broad basin was scooped out, forming the now famous "horseshoe" of Niagara Falls.

DETAIL OF CATLINITE CLIFF, PIPE-
STONE NATIONAL MONUMENT,
PIPESTONE, MINNESOTA

*An ancient catlinite quarry in the
southwest corner of Minnesota is the
site of a thousand years of sacred
pipe carving by the Ojibway, Lakota,
Cheyenne and Blackfoot tribes,
among others. Both history and legend
refer to Pipestone as a holy ground
where warring nations would put
down their arms and smoke the pipe
together, united in reverence for the
Great Spirit. Today, Pipestone
remains a meeting place revered by
many First Nations people, and
almost all the pipes used in ceremony
by North America's Native people
come from the quarries here, though
much of the remaining rock is hidden
under ten to thirteen feet of quartzite.*

PIPESTONE ◆ QUARRY OF PEACE

LAKOTA LEGEND

One Lakota story speaks of the deep crimson stone as being the hardened blood of those
crushed in a great flood. Another says that the first pipe was brought to the ancestors by
White Buffalo Calf Woman, a messenger from the Great Spirit, thus forming a link
between those on Earth and those in the spirit world. She taught them that the pipe—the
bowl engraved with a buffalo calf—joins land and sky, and its smoke carries messages to
the Great Spirit. She showed them how to pray with the pipe, how to decorate themselves
when praying to Mother Earth, and above all else, to use it as a peace pipe to be smoked
before all ceremonies. She taught them the seven sacred rites, including the Inipi (the
cleansing sweat lodge), the Wiwanyaq Wachipi (the sundance of thanksgiving) and the
Ishuata Awicalowan (the ceremony to prepare a girl for womanhood). In this last ritual,
the girl is honored like a towering tree; she is a source of strength and, like the Mother
Earth, will bear children, raising them in a spiritual way.

PETROGLYPHS IN SUNSET LIGHT, JEFFERS PETROGLYPH SITE, JEFFERS, MINNESOTA

Petroglyph art is believed to have served many purposes: it played a role in sacred ceremonies, it helped people remember events and it recorded important occurrences. Some designs appear to be clan symbols, while others identify the best places to hunt, the location and strength of an enemy, or a favored migration route.

Of the 203 clusters of carvings at Jeffers, some may date from 3000 B.C. These older carvings portray magic hunting rituals, with depictions of ancient spears. Others date from 900 A.D. to as recent as 1750, when the Siouan-speaking peoples first used the horse in this area.

The bison, a dominant figure in these carvings, is known to possess a particular magic for the Plains Indians. The serpent also appears with frequency; to many Native cultures it is a symbol of potent life energy and universal knowledge.

RED ROCK RIDGE • PLACE OF ANCIENT CARVINGS

While there are petroglyphs at many sites throughout North America, there are few locations with as diverse and extensive a collection as the two thousand carvings at Jeffers Petroglyph Site on Red Rock Ridge. A short distance east of Pipestone in southwestern Minnesota, this thousand-foot mural of ancient artwork can be found on a twenty-three-mile ridge above game trails that follow the Cottonwood River. Little is actually known about either the origin or the meaning of these quartzite etchings, though many of the figures are thought to have spiritual significance. The ridge is, however, an enchanting place to explore, especially when the figures transform to gold in the low light of a clear evening.

BUTTERFLY AND LICHEN ON QUARTZITE,
JEFFERS PETROGLYPH SITE, JEFFERS, MINNESOTA

RINGING ROCKS · HARMONY OF THE EARTH

UNAMI LEGEND

This area of what is now Pennsylvania was originally inhabited by the Unami- and Munsee-speaking people, who lived in agricultural and hunting villages. Although much remains unknown about their beliefs, the Unami name means "original person," and their stories speak of a Cannibal Monster and of the Thunderers, winged spirits who protect the world from the enemy, Great Horned Serpent. Other benevolent beings were the Little People, who lived in the woods, as well as "our Older Brother the Sun" and "our Mother the Earth."

The descendants of the Unami people were the Delaware tribes, named in the seventeenth century to honor the region's first English governor, Lord de la Warr. With European settlement, the Delaware people were driven west to Oklahoma and north to Canada, where they have since been absorbed by the Indian peoples in those areas.

BOULDERS AND TREES,
RINGING ROCKS STATE PARK, PENNSYLVANIA

Nestled in a grove of woods near Upper Black Eddy on the Delaware River lies a clearing strewn with boulders that have a special history. Although the glaciers did not reach this far, a unique paraglacial climate that lasted here until about 7000 B.C. produced periods of freezing and thawing. This allowed volcanic intrusions to heat and crack the bedrock, leaving rivers of rock.

The uncanny sense of mystery and spirit that pervades this place is heightened by the unique musical quality of its rocks. The bowl-shaped indentations in this malleable shale are the results of decades of visitors attempting to hear the ringing; when struck with a hammer or small stone, the boulders resound, their crystalline nature producing characteristic tones.

DETAIL OF COILS, SERPENT MOUND, SERPENT MOUND STATE MEMORIAL, OHIO

SERPENT MOUND • EFFIGY OF UNSEEN POWER

To many North American Indian people, the serpent is a manifestation of the life energy force and of unseen power. Some anthropologists believe that Serpent Mound represents a solar eclipse, with the egg shape symbolizing the sun about to be swallowed by the snake. We may never know for certain what the ancient valley dwellers intended to portray.

The serpent plays an important role in other cultures as well. In the ancient Quechua language of South America, the Western Hemisphere is called "Amaruka," or "land of the serpent." Many Toltec and Mayan temples in Mexico are adorned with snake carvings, indicating a place of wisdom. To the Hindus, the serpent means enlightenment; to the Christians, forbidden knowledge; to the Greeks, it was the life force symbol on the physician's staff; and to the Chinese metaphysicians practicing the art of Feng Shui (geomancy, or the ancient science of earth energies), the serpent force is the energy that circulates not only in the human body but also through the earth. It may be significant that this Serpent Mound is near a creek; perhaps these early builders believed, as do modern geomancers, that the presence of water increases the electromagnetic forces in the earth.

PAGES 28–29

AERIAL VIEW OF SERPENT MOUND, SERPENT MOUND STATE MEMORIAL, OHIO

Serpent Mound is an enormous earthen snake that, uncoiled, would measure more than a quarter of a mile. Poised in a grove of trees on a ridge that parallels Ohio Brush Creek near Locust Grove, Ohio, this is the largest serpent effigy in the world. Serpent Mound is believed to have been created sometime between 1000 B.C. and 400 A.D. by people anthropologists call the Adena or the succeeding Hopewell, the latter of which evolved into the Mississippian culture. All three of these Eastern Woodlands peoples, ancestors of present-day North American Indians, built ceremonial and burial mounds. Although thousands of burial mounds exist in North America, predominantly in the Mississippi and Ohio river valleys, and many of the later ones featured extensive temple complexes and walled cities, the Serpent Mound emerges as a particularly fascinating site. Its unique shape and the fact that no human remains were unearthed here imbue it with a sense of continuous mystery.

MATEO TEPEE ◆ DEVIL'S TOWER

KIOWA LEGEND

A Kiowa youth was playing with his seven sisters when he found that he could not speak. His body grew long hair. His fingers and toes grew sharp claws, and he grew bigger and bigger and was thus transformed into a ferocious giant bear. His sisters were terrified. The boy-bear roared and dropped on all fours and chased his sisters. They climbed onto a tree stump and prayed desperately for help. The Great Spirit responded by turning the tree stump into a tower and placing them beyond the ferocious bear's reach. The giant bear raised up to his full height and clawed at the tower with his sharp claws, thus making the vertical streaks on the sides of the tower.

On a clear, still night, the seven sisters can still be seen because they have been transformed into the seven stars of the Big Dipper.

LAKOTA LEGEND

Two boys who lost their way walked aimlessly for three days. Suddenly they saw Mato, the giant grizzly, who chased them. They called out to the Great Spirit to save them. A tremendous earthquake suddenly raised the boys a thousand feet up. Mato, who is enormous, dug his claws into the rock but was unable to reach them. Eventually Mato left, but the boys were stranded on the top of the tower called Bear Rock by the Lakotas.

Some have said that it was Wanblee, the giant eagle, who rescued them.

LAME DEER'S STORY

Lame Deer, a Lakota medicine man born in the late 1890s on the Rosebud Reservation in South Dakota, told the story of a great flood that covered the land and drowned everyone except a beautiful girl. Galeshka, the spotted eagle, picked her up with his enormous claws and took her to the only visible land, the tip of a rocky tower, Mateo Tepee, and made her his wife. She gave birth to twins who became the founders of the great Lakota nation.

It is said that all people are descendants of the eagle, the wisest of birds and the messenger of the Great Spirit.

WEST FACE OF TOWER,
DEVIL'S TOWER NATIONAL MONUMENT, WYOMING

Known today as Devil's Tower in eastern Wyoming, Mateo Tepee is the teardrop-shaped core of an ancient volcano that rises 867 feet from its base. There are several stories about the origin of this monumental land-mark and all of them involve a giant bear.

EASTERN RIDGE, BEAR BUTTE, BLACK HILLS, SOUTH DAKOTA

BEAR BUTTE • SHRINE OF VISION

LAKOTA LEGEND

Lakota oral tradition says that Bear Butte, known as Mato Pah, was formed from the titanic struggle between a huge bear and Uncegila. Both shed blood until the strong and fierce bear—symbol of power and vitality—finally conceded defeat and collapsed. The land convulsed and covered his body with earth. Now he hibernates here forever, the keeper of dreams.

The great Lakota chief, Crazy Horse, came to Bear Butte many times throughout his life. In one vision, he was directed up a bright white path on the eastern ridge toward an arrow-shaped cave, where his body was embedded with several small stones that gave him messages from the Great Spirit, Wakan Tanka, and sent out sparks when he performed healing ceremonies. The eastern meadow is designated as his Teaching Hill, where he spoke to many councils who gathered to receive his direction and wisdom.

CHEYENNE LEGEND

The Cheyenne call Bear Butte Noahvose, meaning the place of Maheo, the Above Spirit. It is here that their great prophet, Sweet Medicine, waited four years before he received the four sacred arrows from the Great Spirit. The sacred arrows contained Maheo's teachings, including the four taboos—murder, theft, adultery and incest. Sweet Medicine took the sacred bundle of arrows and used their powers to show his people a spiritual way to live.

Cheyenne and Lakota stories speak of a time before any hills existed in this part of South Dakota, when humans and fellow creatures preyed indiscriminately on each other. Man summoned all to a race in the path of great circle, where everyone participated in a frenzied commotion that disturbed the spirits. As the path wore the earth away, it began to sink, and the land within the circle rose up to form a mountainous bulge that burst. Many were killed, including the monster Uncegila, whose bones can be found on the ridges of the Badlands. The Black Hills, at the center of this cataclysm, are a reminder to humans that their strength is insignificant compared to the awesome power of the earth spirits.

MAKO SICA • BADLANDS OF THE WHITE RIVER

LEGEND OF THE UNCEGILA

It was here in Mako Sica that Uncegila, a female water monster, emerged from the primordial sea and flooded the land, bringing devastation to the people. Wakinyan, the frightful and awe-inspiring Thunderbird, was angered and worried that there would be no people to pray to him or to dream of his great powers. So Wakinyan created a violent storm, flapping his wings to produce thunderbolts that dried up the flood and destroyed the vengeful Uncegila. Her red crystal heart shattered, but her bones remain scattered in the Badlands as a testament to the power of the spirits.

John Lame Deer, a Lakota elder, tells another story. While looking for lost horses, he grew fearful and could feel the ground shaking as though Uncegila were wriggling beneath him, her bones protruding from a ridge of red and yellow rocks. Taking refuge from a storm, Lame Deer heard Wakinyan giving him encouragement. When he later tried to find the horses and the ridge site, they had vanished.

SAGE CREEK WILDERNESS AREA, BADLANDS NATIONAL PARK, SOUTH DAKOTA

Many fossils have been found in the Badlands, an area once covered by an inland sea. It has been a hunting ground for more than twelve thousand years. First used by ancient mammoth hunters, this tortuous land was later occupied by the Arikara people, and then by the Lakota, who named it Mako Sica and hunted bison here. It is said that this is a good place to hide; the last ghost dancers took refuge here in 1890, when the Ghost Dance was banned by the U.S. government. Today, it is the home of the Oglala Sioux, who oversee the administration of Badlands National Park.

ROCK EAGLE • MYSTERY OF THE STONE MOUND CULTURE

In many Native traditions, animals are seen as spiritual messengers that instruct through dreams or trances. The eagle is often symbolic of a shaman's journey to communicate with the spirit world.

Little is known for sure about this effigy, although it is thought by some to have been a guardian spirit for the Eagle Clan and used by them as a ceremonial center. The Creek and Cherokee people who currently live in the area say their ancestors found the Rock Eagle as it is today, and they have no knowledge of its use. It seems clear that it was a site of great spiritual importance, since the large rocks used in its construction were brought from a great distance without the benefit of wheeled transportation or horses.

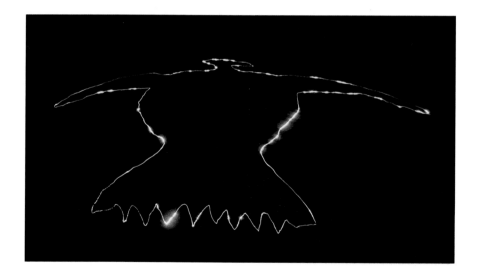

FLASHLIGHT TRACING AT NIGHT, ROCK EAGLE EFFIGY, EATONTON, GEORGIA

ROCK EAGLE EFFIGY IN DAWN MIST,
EATONTON, GEORGIA

*Rock Eagle, an enormous bird effigy with a 120-foot wingspan, is
located near Eatonton, Georgia. Constructed entirely from white quartz
boulders, it would seem to have been built five thousand years ago,
making it older than the Great Pyramid of Egypt. The Mississippian
people, ancestors of the Native people who live here today, constructed
many burial and effigy mounds in this area between 1000 and 1500
A.D. and may be descended from the people who built Rock Eagle.*

SOUTH

To the South, and thy sentinel, Brown Eagle / The beautiful one, grant us warmth of heart, / Love and kindness to all.

PAHAYOKEE • RIVER OF GRASSY WATERS

SEMINOLE LORE

The Milky Way was created by the Breathmaker, who blew toward the sky to make a pathway to the City of the West, where good souls go after death. It is said that Rain and Rainbow (or "Stop-The-Rain") live along this path, and that the Big Dipper is the boat that carries good souls away, while bad ones stay in the ground where they are buried.

Ancient stories refer to a special collaboration between alligators and humans. In one Choctaw story, a stranded alligator asks for assistance and returns the favor of his human helper by pointing out good deer-hunting spots.

OPPOSITE:
ALLIGATOR AND REFLECTION, ANHINGA TRAIL, EVERGLADES NATIONAL PARK, FLORIDA

LEFT:
MANGROVE REFLECTION, PEARL BAY, EVERGLADES NATIONAL PARK, FLORIDA

Prior to the arrival of Europeans, the swamps of Florida were inhabited for more than two thousand years by the Tequesta and Calusa Indians, who called them Pahayokee (pay-HIGH-oh-geh), "the grassy waters." To the Spanish explorers who arrived here in the late fifteenth century, this was a mysterious place they called "lagoon of the Holy Spirit." Only since the 1820s have these eight million acres of water, mangrove, cypress, sawgrass and rushes been called "the Everglades," so named by the British because they thought the shiny green marshland went on forever.

SPIRO MOUNDS • SITE OF ANCIENT BURIAL

SOUTHERN CULT PRACTICES

Archaeological remnants give evidence of ceremonial activities based on ritual, militarism and the unique burial practices of the Southern cult, a tradition of religious beliefs, symbols and priestly leadership. When a tribal leader died, the body was allowed to decompose so that the bones could be buried in a communal underground chamber. There the honored bones were surrounded by ceremonial pipes, shell masks, copper-covered earspools, engraved pottery, axes, baskets, knives and copper plates embossed with intricate designs.

OPPOSITE:
COMPOSITE OF LIGHT REFRACTION THROUGH
QUARTZ CRYSTAL AND SILHOUETTE OF CRAIG MOUND,
SPIRO MOUNDS STATE PARK, OKLAHOMA

In what is now the northeast corner of Oklahoma, a group of large burial mounds gives testimony to the area's original inhabitants, the Wichita and Caddoan tribes. This thousand-year-old site, now called Spiro Mounds, was a major ceremonial and trade center. It controlled movement on the Arkansas River from the western plains to villages in the southeast woodlands until about 1350, when it is speculated that climatic changes brought about a devastating drought, driving people to the southern plains to hunt buffalo.

From time to time, eerie blue lights have been reported over Craig Mound, the largest multiple burial mound on this site, where excavations have revealed 189 burial units with evidence of at least nine successive layers of building. Scientists have suggested that the lights may be the result of interaction between the large number of copper objects found in the mound and natural gas radiating from the surface. Many quartz crystals have also been found buried at Spiro, perhaps used by shamans to look into the future.

41 SOUTH

HOT WATER CASCADE, HOT
SPRINGS NATIONAL PARK,
ARKANSAS

The healing medicinal waters of
Hot Springs, heated to 143°,
have taken four thousand years
to form before reaching the surface,
where they gush at a rate of
850,000 gallons a day to
numerous springs seeping through
a fracture zone on the western
edge of Hot Springs Mountain.

HOT SPRINGS • VALLEY OF THE VAPORS

TUNICA LEGEND

The Tunica believe their people originated in these thermal springs. The vapors of the hot springs were said to be the breath of the Great Spirit, who favored the hot springs and the surrounding mountains as a retreat. Another story tells of a dragon named Mogmothon, who brought sickness, hunger and devastation to the people of this land. A council of Indian nations met and prayed to the Great Spirit to help them; their prayer was answered and the beast was hurled into a cave. But even when buried by the mountain, the dragon could still shake the ground and cause thunderstorms. As a sign of his power and goodness, the Great Spirit brought forth the healing waters to remind his people to live in peace, and to maintain this beloved spot as a neutral place to partake in life- and health-giving activities.

LICHEN DETAIL, HOT SPRINGS MOUNTAIN, HOT SPRINGS NATIONAL PARK, ARKANSAS

In addition to the therapeutic mineral waters, Hot Springs is noted for the intricately patterned lichen and moss and the exquisitely colored rock in its vicinity. Thick accumulations of chert, known as novaculite, have been quarried here for centuries by Native peoples and carved for tools, arrow-points and spearheads. Europeans later used novaculite to fashion whet-stones. This unique geological area also produces some of the finest white crystal rocks on the continent, often used as healing stones by shamans past and present.

DETAIL OF REFRACTED LIGHT IN QUARTZ CRYSTAL, QUARTZ MINE, ARKANSAS

MANITOU SPRINGS • PLACE OF GATHERING

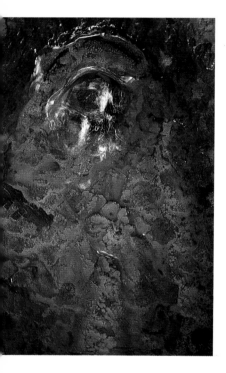

UTE LEGEND

According to Ute stories, the natural effervescence of these springs is the result of Manitou breathing into them, so the waters were named in honor of this Great Spirit.

Adjacent to Manitou Springs is a fourteen-hundred-acre park now called the Garden of the Gods, but known to Native people as "the Old Red Lands." Here several tribes would gather amidst the elegant spires, jagged pinnacles and spirit faces in the rock. For the Ute, it was also a sacred place where elders climbed the cliffs and wedged themselves into crevices until they passed over to the other world. Their bodies would then be removed to the nearby burial ground.

JICARILLA APACHE LEGEND

The Jicarilla Apache, who lived in these mountains as early as 1000 A.D., tell how the moaning created by wind swirling at the front of the cavern was like the voice of the Great Spirit who lived there. In order to avoid disturbing and angering the Great Spirit, no one entered the cave.

ABOVE:
DETAIL OF OPENING, IRON SPRINGS, MANITOU SPRINGS, COLORADO

RIGHT:
SILHOUETTE OF UNIDENTI-FIED ROCK, GARDEN OF THE GODS, MANITOU SPRINGS, COLORADO

WHITE ROCK, NORTH GATEWAY AND PIKES PEAK (DISTANT), GARDEN OF THE GODS,
MANITOU SPRINGS, COLORADO

Nestled in a valley on the eastern edge of Pikes Peak in present-day Colorado, Manitou Springs is a network of twenty-six mineral fountains. The Ute Indians, whose culture dates back ten thousand years and continues to thrive, used the mountain trail now known as the Ute Pass to travel from Colorado Springs to their wintering camps on the western plains.

By the late 1800s, the Native tribes in this area were forced to move to reservations in the Four Corners region, where the states of Utah, Arizona, New Mexico and Colorado intersect. Pikes Peak swarmed with settlers and gold mines, while the springs became a tourist attraction. Today, all the springs are capped and most are piped to the surface in the form of fountains. While the natural ambience is lost, local people say that the spiritual magnetism of this area still exists.

ENCHANTED ROCK • DOME OF THE SUPERNATURAL

TONKAWA TRADITION

Ancient peoples have lived in this area of central Texas for eleven thousand years, from the nomadic spear throwers who hunted the woolly mammoth, to the later (900–1700 A.D.) hunting-and-gathering nations who used to bow and arrow to bring down bison. Their descendants, the nomadic Tonkawa, had a great respect for death; they buried their dead with the head facing west, believing that the spirit departs in that direction in the form of an owl or wolf. The strange sounds emitted from within enchanted Rock were attributed to the dead, and the Tonkawa thought that if the spirits haunted a place, those nearby could be tainted and die.

APACHE LEGACY

Enchanted Rock's legacy includes a stirring account of an Apache elder who instructs a youth to listen to the spirit here—not to his brothers—because what is learned from the mountain will endure forever.

OPPOSITE:
ENCHANTED ROCK, WEST FACE, POST-SUNSET LIGHT, ENCHANTED ROCK
STATE NATIONAL AREA, TEXAS

BELOW:
GRANITE SLABS ON LITTLE ROCK, ENCHANTED ROCK STATE NATIONAL AREA,
TEXAS

By day, Enchanted Rock lures the hiker to explore the valleys, creeks, fissures, caves and oblong slabs of rock draped on the exterior of this pink granite dome. By night, it taunts visitors with its mysterious cracking sounds and deep crimson glow.

Today, there are some who see Enchanted Rock as a doorway to the other side of existence. Shamans and medicine people still come here to practice their art and to connect with the spirit world.

DETAIL OF TRAVERTINE
RESIDUE ON SIDE OF
FOUNTAIN, PAGOSA
SPRINGS, COLORADO

*Although much of the site's
natural atmosphere has been
destroyed, colorful mineral
encrustations, called travertine,
can be seen in a fountain in
the town square and flowing
down the nearby banks of the
San Juan River.*

PAHGASA • BOILING WATERS

UTE LEGEND

Pagosa Springs, Colorado, gets its name from the Ute word Pahgasa, meaning "boiling waters." During a time of plague, when even the medicine people failed to stop the deaths, a tribal council built a giant bonfire, then danced and beseeched the gods for help. They slept, and upon awakening they found the bonfire replaced with a pool of boiling water, a gift from the Great Spirit who healed them of their sickness.

TEWA PUEBLO LEGEND

To the Tewa Pueblo people of Arizona, Pagosa Springs was known as Warm Sands, a place of winter pilgrimage, and a story is told of two Tewa Pueblo men who, driving north on their way to a sundance, stopped, knelt on the sand and were overcome by memories of distant ancestors. They had never been there before, yet they felt a powerful homecoming.

No rivers are seen now at the site of Three Rivers Petroglyphs, north of Tularosa, New Mexico, but there remains an abundance of superbly carved figures in the rock outcroppings. Archaeologists believe the carvings were made more than six hundred years ago by people they call the Jornada branch of the Mogollon culture, descendants of those who inhabited New Mexico from about 5000 B.C.

THREE RIVERS • PETROGLYPHS OF MYSTERY

Three Rivers is the site of one of the largest collections of petroglyphs in North America, with nearly twenty thousand carvings of birds, insects, animals, hands, masks, human figures, suns, moons, stars, crosses, circles, geometric designs and anthropomorphic beings.

Some of these ancient petroglyph figures seem to depict the type of game that roamed this fertile valley in abundance, while others may record great events in people's lives. What the majority of the carvings have in common is their mystical quality. Images of faces and masks abound at Three Rivers. Facing Sierra Blanca, a mountain sacred to the Apache, is one of the most prominent carvings which depicts a large face with almond-shaped eyes and an inverted mouth full of jaguar-shaped teeth. These teeth are drawn in a fringelike design similar to the Tlaloc masks on the Temple of Quetzalcoatl at Teotihuacan, Mexico. Tlaloc was an important deity, "he who makes things grow," and as one of the most ancient gods of Mesoamerica, he lived on the mountain surrounded by clouds, where he controlled the all-important rains.

PETROGLYPH RESEMBLING
TLALOC MASK AND SIERRA
BLANCA, PETROGLYPH SITE,
THREE RIVERS, NEW MEXICO

DETAIL OF PETROGLYPH
RESEMBLING "QUETZALCOATL"
SYMBOL, THREE RIVERS PET-
ROGLYPH SITE, THREE RIVERS,
NEW MEXICO

One petroglyph symbol in particular—a cross within a circle with varying numbers of distinct dots around the circumference—occurs repeatedly. While the cross within a circle is a prominent southwestern symbol for the Hopi Sky God, the version with the dots rarely appears at other North American sites. It is, however, seen in diverse forms throughout Mesoamerica as a symbol of the god Quetzalcoatl, and some believe these petroglyphs provide evidence that links three great cultures—the Mexican, the Mogollon and the Pueblo.

PETROGLYPH OF SIX-FINGERED
HANDS, THREE RIVERS PETRO-
GLYPH SITE, THREE RIVERS,
NEW MEXICO

WHITE SANDS • SEA OF ALABASTER

APACHE CREATION STORY
According to the Apache, the Giver of Life warned of a coming deluge and directed White Painted Woman to take refuge in a floating abalone shell. When the waters receded, the shell came to rest at White Sands. There, she gave birth to two children, Son of the Sun and Child of the Water. Also known as Changing Woman, and the greatest cultural hero of the Apache, she teaches how to rid the world of evil. Her youth is eternally renewed, thus symbolizing the continual re-creation of the sands.

PUEBLO LEGEND
A Spaniard named Hernando de Luna, accompanied by his bride-to-be, Manuela, was a scout on a northward expedition led by the infamous conquistador, Coronado. On the edge of the Great White Sands, Apache warriors ambushed the scouts and de Luna was never seen again. It is said that the ghost of the bereaved Manuela, called Pavla Blanca, can be seen following the sunset, her white wedding robes blowing like sand in the wind. To see her once is good luck, twice is bad luck and three times brings death.

OPPOSITE AND ABOVE:
GYPSUM DUNES, WHITE SANDS NATIONAL MONUMENT, NEW MEXICO

Contrasting starkly against the flat prairie and jagged foothills of the San Andreas Mountains, the chalk white sliver of White Sands, New Mexico, can be seen from as far away as the highest trail at Three Rivers, a distance of fifty miles. The dunes of this "alabaster sea" shift ceaselessly over an area of nearly three hundred square miles, and because it is so bright and easily identifiable, White Sands has served as a reference point for thousands of years—for stone-age

hunters following the big-horned bison and for space-age astronauts who can spot the white sand sea from their space capsule.

Composed of particles from an elegant, crystalline form of gypsum called selenite, the sand has been produced for twenty-five thousand years by the annual drying of Lake Lucero, the lowest point in the entire Tularosa Basin and once an inland sea.

VIEW FROM SOUTH RIM, CANYON DE CHELLY NATIONAL
MONUMENT, ARIZONA

Sacred to both Hopi and Navajo, Spider Rock, a thousand-foot-high twin column of sandstone, is the home of Spider Woman, who spins a web that captures and devours misbehaving children who are reported to her by Speaking Rock across the canyon. The white rocks on top of the tower are said to be the sun-bleached bones of the victims.

CANYON DE CHELLY • TEACHINGS OF THE HOLY BEINGS

NAVAJO LEGEND

The Navajo refer to this canyon as "where the water comes out of the rock," and consider it one of their most important ceremonial sites. They believe this is where the Holy Beings taught their people how to live, and that it is also the place to restore harmony to mind and spirit through medicine rituals.

HOPI CREATION STORY

The Hopi emerged from a corrupt Third World into the present Fourth World, where the guardian spirit, Maasaw, revealed their destiny: to live out the Creator's plan and to search for his footprints throughout the valleys, rocks and woods.

DETAIL OF SANDSTONE CLIFF AT WHITE HOUSE RUINS, CANYON DE CHELLY
NATIONAL MONUMENT, ARIZONA

CLIFF DWELLINGS AT BETATAKIN NAVAJO NATIONAL MONUMENT, ARIZONA

Betatakin, meaning "ledge house" in Navajo, lies in Navajo National Monument, northwest of Canyon de Chelly. A harmonious blend of architecture and nature, the cliff dwellings here were constructed on a narrow ledge, protected by an enormous rock overhang and displaying the appearance of an amphitheater, its vaulted ceiling rising eight hundred feet above the valley floor. It is believed to have been inhabited only between 1250 and 1286 A.D.

MESA VERDE • CLIFF PALACE OF ANTIQUITY

ANASAZI CULTURE

While Mesa Verde lies in the center of present-day Ute territory, the ledges of this central plateau harbor a series of ancient cliff dwellings inhabited by the Anasazi. The name Mesa Verde, Spanish for "green table," refers to the fertile soil and hunting conditions on the mesa tops that were densely populated from 900 to 1300 A.D. The Anasazi took advantage of nature and built their communities into the side of the cliff under the protection of sandstone overhangs. Of the five thousand ruins uncovered, the Cliff Palace is one of the most magnificent examples of how the Anasazi fitted their stone construction to the available space and contours of the land. Towers and three-story dwellings surround circular structures called kivas, the Hopi name for underground rooms, which are still used for ceremonies and social gatherings.

The Cliff Palace was occupied for less than one hundred years. Possibly a climatic change forced the Anasazi to move to more fertile areas, leaving these structures empty for more than seven hundred years, like ghosts of an enchanted past.

DOUBLE EXPOSURE OF CLIFF PALACE AND CLIFF FACE, MESA VERDE NATIONAL PARK, COLORADO

From the high plateau country of southwestern Colorado, one can see many sacred landscapes. To the north, the La Plata Mountains mark the boundary of the Navajo Nation; to the south, the "Rock of Wings," known as Shiprock or Tse Bit'a'i, is the home of the Winged Monsters of Navajo history; and to the west, Sleeping Ute Mountain is the place where Ute stories say the Rain God gathered all the clouds in his pocket.

ABOVE:
SILHOUETTE OF PUEBLO BONITO, CHACO CULTURE
NATIONAL HISTORIC PARK, NEW MEXICO

OPPOSITE:
"LUNAR NECKLACE," MULTIPLE EXPOSURE OF MOON
AND CASA RINCONADA (FISHEYE LENS), CHACO CUL-
TURE NATIONAL HISTORIC PARK, NEW MEXICO

CHACO CANYON • CENTER OF ANASAZI CULTURE

HOPI RITUALS

Although each community had many kivas, the ritual functions of Chaco are believed to have taken place in Casa Rinconada, the largest kiva in the valley. For the Hopi, who believe their ancestors passed through here, this round, underground ceremonial room symbolizes the womb of the Earth Mother, where man emerged from the underworld. Hopi stories also identify Chaco as one of the stops their ancestors made on the long migration, following the footsteps of Maasaw to their home on the Three Mesas to the west. Today, Hopi communities continue to use kivas for ceremonies, often involving drumming and dancing. It seems certain that this kiva was the Anasazi link with the cosmos; its two outer entrances are built on a north-south axis, directly in line with celestial north and congruent with the four cardinal directions.

NAVAJO LORE

Navajo oral histories of Chaco Canyon say that it was here that the Holy People won back all their property from the Great Gambler, who was then exiled to the sky. Although scientists suggest that a change in climate precipitated the Anasazi's departure, Navajo stories teach that the Ancient Ones were dispersed by a whirlwind because they had abandoned the ways of their ancestors.

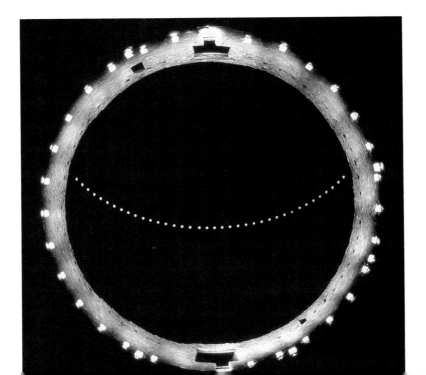

OPPOSITE:
"DOORS," PUEBLO BONITO, CHACO
CULTURE NATIONAL HISTORIC PARK,
NEW MEXICO

*In Pueblo Bonito, the doorways align
with each other, creating a feeling of
transformation as you pass from room
to room, like a rebirth into successive
spiritual worlds.*

RIGHT:
PUEBLO BONITO FROM ABOVE, CHACO
CULTURE NATIONAL HISTORIC PARK,
NEW MEXICO

*Chaco Canyon was perhaps the greatest
seat of power of the Anasazi culture,
which flourished here between 900 and
1300 A.D. Pueblo Bonito, a city complex
of eight hundred rooms and thirty-two
kivas, is nestled in the base of the eastern
cliffs at a major crossroads in the canyon.
Archaeologists believe it was the center of
a large trade network comprised of seventy
or eighty surrounding villages, and
accessible by four hundred miles of well-
built roadways. However, more recent
investigations using aerial remote sensing
techniques suggest that Pueblo Bonito may
have been Chaco's major ceremonial
center—the legendary "Middle Place" of
the Anasazi spiritual world—with more
than a thousand miles of roads over an
area of sixty thousand square miles. This
classic Anasazi period is identified by
multi-story villages that were sustained
by irrigation and supported by a vast
distribution network.*

ANTELOPE CANYON • RAINBOW OF THE EARTH

NAVAJO LORE

Local Navajo people say that their ancestors, the Anasazi, used the canyons as refuge from the elements as well as from their enemies. The canyons have sacred significance because they represent the womb from which the Earth Mother gives birth and are believed to be monuments to the life force of the female energy of water. Some Navajo people continue to perform water purification ceremonies here.

The canyons are also believed to be the home of the chindi, wicked spirits who spend most of their time in the afterworld located below the earth, seeking revenge for wrongs done to them during their life. They are barely visible, but sometimes they can be heard making noise while wandering through dark canyon recesses.

OPPOSITE LEFT, OPPOSITE RIGHT AND BELOW: REFLECTED SUNLIGHT ON SANDSTONE FORMATIONS, ANTELOPE CANYON, PAGE, ARIZONA

Near Page, Arizona, is a network of slot canyons that eventually empty into Lake Powell. The best known is Antelope Canyon. If one peers down from ground level into a two-hundred-foot drop, all that is visible is a black fissure in the sandstone, but inside lies a rainbow of color.

Centuries of flash floods have etched out the sweeping shapes of chambers, columns, corridors, sinkholes and caves. In the Navajo language, Tse'neh'na'eh'diz'sjaa means "where water has painted a picture of itself."

NAVAJO MOUNTAIN
AND LAKE POWELL, PAGE,
ARIZONA

From the shores of Lake Powell, on the border of Utah and Arizona, Navajo Mountain emerges through the mist, forty miles to the east. Called Naatsis'aan in Navajo, the mountain is known as "the Head of Earth," the place that brings clouds from the heavens.

NAVAJO MOUNTAIN • HEAD OF THE EARTH

NAVAJO LORE

Navajo stories connect this cloud-making mountain to a rainbow in stone, the nearby sandstone arch called Rainbow Bridge, the Earth's largest natural bridge. For the Navajo, this is the home of the Rainbow People and a place of pilgrimage where correct rituals ensure the coming of life-giving rains. To pass under the bridge without chanting the correct songs is said to bring certain death. The Navajo have many traditional chants, performed to restore physical and spiritual well-being. For example, when the Mountain Healing Song is sung over a person, that person's spirit makes the journey to a holy place beyond the sacred mountain, where it is blessed or healed by the Divine Ones who live there.

A Navajo creation story speaks of Black Body and Blue Body, the first man and woman, who built the mountain with earth brought from the underworld. Geological evidence concurs: the mountain is made up of a lava core that would have turned black and blue as it solidified.

DETAIL OF CANYON WALLS AT
PEACH CANYON, ARIZONA

*Peach Canyon is located on private
Navajo land about thirty miles
southeast of Antelope Canyon.
Almost impassable in some places,
it narrows to a slit with ledges too
tenuous to walk across.*

PEACH CANYON • ABODE OF THE CHINDI

TSE DO NAHU NTI AND TSE AHEENIDITII

Many Navajo stories speak of beasts like tse do nahu nti, the impossible crevice monster, and tse aheeniditii, the crushing rock monster, who live in slot canyons. In one story, the sons of Changing Woman and Father Sun want to destroy the monsters, and they seek their father to help them. Their journey takes them through the canyon that crushes, where Spider Woman advises them to chant special prayers. She also provides magic feathers that protect them from the crashing walls and allow them to escape and continue their quest.

WIPUK • FOOT OF THE ROCKS

YAVAPAI CREATION LEGEND

According to their creation story, all Yavapai originated at Wipuk. Sakarakaamche taught them how to pray, to sing and to dance. Singing is a form of prayer, passed down through the generations; it connects people with the earth and maintains their vitality. One of Sakarakaamche's songs describes how he descended to Earth on flashes of lightning, sang as he knelt on the ground and caused medicine plants to sprout out of the earth when he lifted his hands. The Yavapai believe that if the songs are not sung and the stories are not told, the land will die.

Another Yavapai story tells that Sedona is the home of the goddess Kamalapukwia, or "grandmother of the supernatural," who lives in a cave. Her grandson, Sakarakaamche, the first man on Earth, possesses great medicine power. Some say that it is he and his grandmother who stand back to back as the dual spires of Cathedral Rock.

LIGHTNING STORM ON MUND'S MOUNTAIN, SEDONA, ARIZONA

MEDICINE WHEEL OVERLOOKING LONG CANYON, SEDONA, ARIZONA

Today, Sedona resembles a huge magnet, attracting people from around the world who yearn to experience the strong earth energies reported here. The land is a catalyst for many emotions; some feel invigorated by the brilliantly burnished red rock, while others find it overpowering and enervating.

The Red Rock country of Sedona was home to Native people as early as ten thousand years ago. The Hohokam and Sinagua people were the ancestors of the Yavapai, the hunter-gatherers who came here in the sixteenth century and called it Wipuk, meaning "at the foot of the rocks." The Yavapai regarded the land with reverence and did not enter the canyons except for ceremonial purposes. In 1875 they were forced from the area, and many perished along the March of Tears to reservations in the east.

EROSIONAL FORMATIONS, BRYCE
CANYON NATIONAL PARK, UTAH

*Bryce Canyon in south-central
Utah cradles some of the most
singular and startling geography
in North America. Geologically it
is the uppermost point of what is
called the Grand Staircase, a series
of cliffs that reflect steps in time,
from the 60 million-year-old Pink
Cliffs that form Bryce, to the 225
million-year-old Kaibab Plateau
that shapes the north rim of the
Grand Canyon, some hundred
miles south. For many, the spires,
turrets, columns and cliffs at Bryce,
which took an eternity to carve,
are awe-inspiring.*

*Bryce is actually not a canyon
at all but a huge amphitheater
sculpted by rain, snow and ice.*

"MOONRISE OVER BRYCE," EROSIONAL FORMATIONS, BRYCE CANYON NATIONAL PARK, UTAH

BRYCE CANYON • PLACE OF THE LEGEND PEOPLE

PAIUTE LEGEND

The Paiute Indians who lived here gave Bryce Canyon a name that translates to "red rocks standing like men in a bowl-shaped canyon." According to a Paiute story, before there were any Indians, this place was inhabited by Legend People called To-when-an-ung-wa, who looked partly like people and partly like birds, animals, or reptiles. For some reason, the Legend People in that place were bad, so Coyote turned them all into rocks. You can see them now, some standing in rows, some sitting down, some holding onto others, their faces painted just as they were before they became rocks.

ECHO CANYON, ZION
NATIONAL PARK, UTAH

This land is steeped in human history. The early Basketmakers and Anasazi were followed by the Paiute, who feared and respected the powerful spirits of the land. More recently, the Ute and Navajo displaced the Paiute. In 1909 the area was proclaimed a National Monument and named Mukuntuweap, the Paiute word for "straight canyon," but it was renamed Zion only two years later, in reference to the early Mormon settlers who saw it as their Heavenly City of God. In spring, the walls of Zion are festooned with greenery and flowers that entice one to the Temple of Sinawava at the head of the canyon.

MUKUNTUWEAP · PLACE WHERE SPIRITS LURK

PAIUTE LEGEND

Here the Wolf God of the Paiute still triumphs in the natural amphitheater named in his honor. But even though the Wolf God was a friendly deity, it is said that his power was not great enough to subdue the evil forces that lurk in The Narrows; this continuation of Zion Canyon is a dead-end chasm called I-oo-goon, meaning "arrow quiver" or "the place where one must come out the same way he went in." Consequently, the Paiute were careful not to be caught here at night.

WEEPING ROCK, ZION
NATIONAL PARK, UTAH

At Weeping Rock, a prominent landmark in Zion Canyon, an underground spring continuously feeds the cliff face with rivulets that fall like teardrops from the overhang.

CLIFF FACE, CABLE MOUNTAIN,
ZION NATIONAL PARK, UTAH

*Many of the other natural monuments at
Zion have been endowed with names that
reflect their inspirational qualities, such as
Great White Throne, Angel's Landing and
The Altar of Sacrifice, referring to the red
wash of color on the rocks.*

RIGHT:
JOSHUA TREES, JOSHUA TREE
NATIONAL MONUMENT,
CALIFORNIA

BELOW:
PALM FROND, COTTONWOOD
SPRINGS, JOSHUA TREE
NATIONAL MONUMENT,
CALIFORNIA

TWENTY-NINE PALMS • OASIS OF FERTILITY

SERRANO LORE

The Serrano (Spanish for "highlander") Indian name for Twenty-Nine Palms is Marrah, the place of "little springs and much grass." One story tells that the Serrano people originally came from the San Bernadino Mountains, where the women gave birth mainly to female babies. The Medicine Man told them that in order to produce males they should go east to the desert, set up camp where there was water, and each time a male was born, plant a tree. In the first year they planted twenty-nine palms.

To the Serrano Indians, the drooping fronds of the palm trees harbor evil spirits that can be heard at night in the rustling of the wind. In the past, they would set the palms on fire, hoping to drive the spirits away, and in so doing, would burn away the dead fronds and underbrush, thus allowing a new cycle of life to begin at the oasis.

Because of the paucity of rain in the desert, oases are crucially important to its animal and human inhabitants. At Joshua Tree, there are four palm oases, each with a natural supply of underground water. One is Twenty-Nine Palms, whose name has been adopted by the town that has grown around it.

California's Joshua Tree National Monument is an unusual desert area characterized most visibly by the many Joshua trees that grow here. The Joshua tree is actually a variety of the yucca plant and grows only in North America's southwestern deserts, sometimes liv-ing for hundreds of years. Since it is the only kind of tree that can survive on the open desert, it is an important source of life for a highly complex ecosystem that includes birds, insects, snakes and desert rodents. In the past, the Serrano, Cahuilla and Chemehuevi people who lived here ate the flowers and the nutritious seeds of the Joshua tree. The Mormons who traveled in this region held it in high esteem because the limbs looked like the welcoming outstretched arms of the prophet Joshua, a sign to them that they were near their "promised land."

WEST

To the West and the Thunder Bird / Who flies over the universe hidden in a cloak of / Rain clouds and cleanses the world of filth, /
Cleanse our bodies and souls of all evil things

SUNFLOWERS AND HILLS AT PAINTED ROCK, CARRIZO PLAIN, CALIFORNIA

Located in the San Joaquin Valley of southern California is a 180,000-acre wildlife reserve with a rich array of wildflowers, endangered species of plants and animals and a migratory bird sanctuary. In its midst lies a holy place called Painted Rock, a massive sandstone monolith that rises 150 feet above the plain.

PAINTED ROCK • PLACE OF WARNING

CHUMASH TRADITION

In the past, the Chumash and Yokut people came to this valley for its game-rich grasslands, trading and tribal rituals. A corridor inside Painted Rock contains an amphitheater of paintings that depict great cosmological events. This rock is an important part of the spiritual life and culture of the Chumash people and is still used for sacred ceremonies.

In a local story that links this place with Mesoamerican traditions, the Dreamer, a High Priest of the Feathered Serpent, once spoke to all people about love, charity, humility and the coming of the great Messiah, Quetzalcoatl.

PAINTED ROCK, CARRIZO PLAIN, CALIFORNIA

PAINTED CAVE • GALLERY OF ROCK ART

CHUMASH BELIEF

Made by Barbareno Chumash artists about one thousand years ago, these paintings are believed to have been part of ritual ceremonies at sacred sites, performed by members of a powerful group of shamans who may have been inspired by vision-inducing substances such as the white flowers of the datura plant. The rock art was created to link the Chumash with sacred events in their past, to maintain balance between supernatural forces in nature and to manipulate supernatural power. One of the paintings, a black circle outlined in white, is thought to depict the November 24, 1677 solar eclipse that would have been visible to the Chumash people of this area, for whom the sun was the most important cosmological element.

Local Native historians have said that Indians in the past would avoid the cave because some of the paintings are thought to represent funerary boats carrying the dead to nearby island graves.

PICTOGRAPHS ON WALL OF PAINTED CAVE, SAN MARCOS PASS, CALIFORNIA

Painted Cave lies twenty-six hundred feet above sea level in the rugged Santa Ynez Mountains of southern California. Although it seems well protected, its sandstone surface has been eroded by the wind, leaving only five feet remaining of the original twenty-one-foot panel. Human destruction has also caused great damage. Graffiti and gunshots have left their marks on what some consider the finest rock art in North America. A heavy metal grate now protects the paintings.

SANDPIPERS IN SETTING
SUN, CONCEPTION
POINT, CALIFORNIA

*Known to the Chumash
Indians as Humqaq, "a
wild and stormy place,"
Conception Point is the
tip of an isthmus of land
that extends into the Pacific
Ocean, northwest of Santa
Barbara, California. This site
is considered the Western Gate
of the continent, where souls
enter and exit the earth.*

HUMQAQ • GATEWAY TO THE ETERNAL

CHUMASH LEGEND

The Chumash are the guardians of this gateway, and Humqaq is the legendary halfway
house to which the soul of the deceased retreats before making the final journey on the
bridge to Similaqsa, the afterworld. Chumash stories tell of the steep cliff at Humqaq,
which can be reached only by rope and which has a basin fed by fresh water. Here the
spirit of the dead is said to paint itself in preparation for the journey across the waters
that separate this world from the next. When the spirit sees the light in the west, it is
ready to make the transition. The eloquent and detailed account of the transition includes
a stage at which the soul travels through a ravine of clashing rocks and is confronted on
either side by two birds called qaq, who peck out its eyes. It replaces them with poppies so
that it can once again see, crosses the last bridge and is finally safe, living forever in abundance and perpetual youth. It is said that sometimes a soul can be seen on its journey, as a
light with a blue trail, and that the gates of Similaqsa can be heard closing behind it like
the sound of a cannon.

PINNACLES ◆ PLACE OF THE GREAT DIVIDE

For the past two thousand years, the Mutsum-speaking people lived to the east of these towering mounds, while the Chalon-speaking people occupied the area to the west. The land is a unique example of a chaparral ecosystem that supports four distinct plant communities and the animals and birds that are attracted to them. The lower-level streams are a source of year-round water, while the upper rock and scree support ninety species of lichen and provide nesting sites for birds such as the endangered California condor. It is not hard to understand how the people of this area viewed the natural world, often referring to the eagle, coyote, falcon, hawk, condor, owl, fox, deer and raven as the "first people" in the history of their culture.

DETAIL OF FOOTHILL WOODLANDS, JUNIPER CANYON, PINNACLES NATIONAL MONUMENT, CALIFORNIA

MOON OVER PINNACLES, PINNACLES NATIONAL MONUMENT, CALIFORNIA

VIEW OF GABILAN RANGE FROM HIGH PEAKS TRAIL, PINNACLES NATIONAL MONUMENT, CALIFORNIA

The history of Pinnacles National Monument is as startling as its monolithic, seemingly endless peaks. The peaks were born 23 million years ago from the lava flow of a volcano positioned between two layers of Earth's crust known as the Pacific and the North American plates. As the volcanic mountain of Pinnacles was formed, the Pacific plate began drifting to the northwest, and millions of years later left behind a portion of these rhyolitic spires 195 miles to the south. This same plate movement created the San Andreas Fault, a rift zone reaching north from the Mendocino coast of San Francisco and south to the Gulf of Mexico. It continues to produce substantial movements even today as the two underground plates of Earth grind against each other.

BODEGA BAY • WHERE THE MOON FALLS DOWN

EASTERN TRIBES LORE
To the Indians of many eastern tribes, the moon is seen as a woman. She has three faces: the crescent moon as a young maiden, the full moon as a mature mother and the new moon or dark moon as an old woman.

SNOQUALMIE LORE
By contrast, for many West Coast Native peoples, the moon is masculine. The Snoqualmie people in Washington have a story that the moon, called Snoqualmie, or Chief of the Heavens, fell down and became a mountain. So important is the moon to all the Indian of North America that their traditional way of measuring time is by its cycles.

BODEGA TRIBE RITUALS
The Bodega tribe of the Coastal Miwok culture who lived here held ceremonies in which spirits of bears and birds were impersonated, with special rituals for the condor and flicker. Birds were captured and reared in their camps to provide feathers for the chief to wear, after which they were released in a ceremony of song and dance.

OPPOSITE:
MULTIPLE EXPOSURES OF MOON SETTING AT GOAT ROCK, BODEGA BAY, CALIFORNIA

Time seems to stand still at Bodega Bay, California, where the morning mists, the sultry sun and the pounding surf lull one into a dream world. By night, the full moon casts a mystical glow on the rising tidal waters, silhouetting Goat Rock in stark relief.

NOTE:

The next-to-last exposure strays from the descending arc because a deer, in its attempt to lick the salty coating on the camera back, bumped the tripod during exposure.

MOUNT SHASTA • LODGE OF THE GREAT SPIRIT

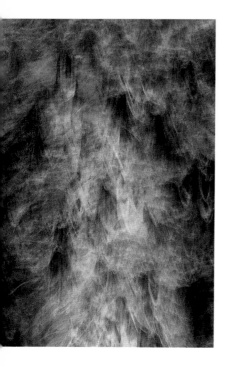

KAROK LORE
A Karok chief told his people to build a mountain high enough to see the sea. When they finished, they emptied their baskets of leftover earth onto the plains below. These are the hundreds of little hills in Shasta Valley.

MODOC LORE
The Chief of the Sky Spirits grew so weary of his icy home in the Above World that he carved a hole in the sky and emptied out all the ice and snow, forming an immense mound known today as Mount Shasta. This lengthy creation story goes on to explain how he formed the trees, rivers, animals and rocky paths, endowing all the features of the mountain with spiritual significance.

SHASTA LEGEND
A Shasta story accounts for Thumb Rock, a projection at the eastern end of the Red Banks. It is thought to be the pointed thumb of an Indian princess who disobeyed her father, the chief, and ran away up the mountain, only to freeze to death there. The message of this story is that the mountain should never be climbed. Native people today still heed that warning and do not climb it, although some lower slopes, such as Panther Meadows, are used for spiritual ceremonies.

ABOVE:
COMPOSITE OF MOVEMENT ON MOSS-CLAD SPRUCE, WESTERN SLOPE, MOUNT SHASTA, CALIFORNIA

RIGHT:
TRIPLE EXPOSURE OF WILD-FLOWERS ON MOUNT SHASTA, CALIFORNIA

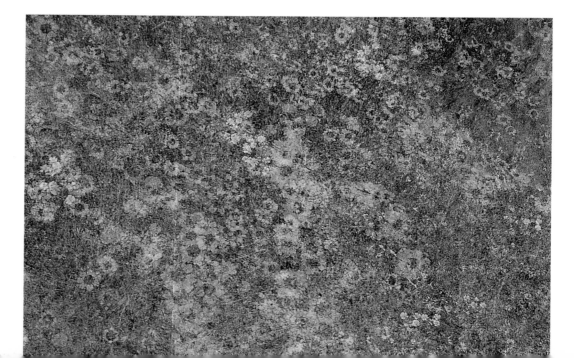

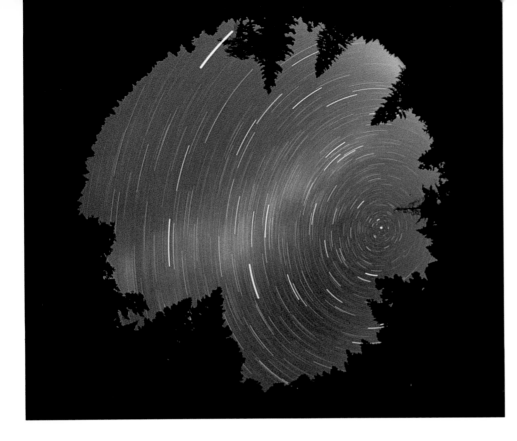

"SKY-HOLE," ONE-HOUR EXPO-
SURE OF STARS (FISHEYE LENS),
MOUNT SHASTA, CALIFORNIA

BELOW:
VIEW FROM THE WEST, MOUNT
SHASTA, CALIFORNIA

*Home to California's largest glaciers,
Mount Shasta stands as a 14,162-
foot beacon at the intersection of three
mountain ranges: the Sierra Nevada
to the southeast, the Cascades to
the north and the Klamath to
the west. This towering volcanic
landmark is revered by the Shasta,
Karok, Modoc and Wintun tribes
of northern California, who
recognize Mount Shasta as a
spiritual center.*

BISON AND FIRE–SWEPT SLOPE, YELLOWSTONE NATIONAL PARK, WYOMING

Yellowstone National Park lies in the northwest corner of Wyoming, 120 miles west of Big Horn Medicine Wheel. Famous for its thermal springs painted with a rainbow of mineral hues, and for its diversity of wildlife, Yellowstone is a natural treasure.

DETAIL OF MINERVA TERRACE, MAMMOTH HOT SPRINGS, YELLOWSTONE, WYOMING

YELLOWSTONE • LAND OF THE GREAT FIRE

CHEYENNE CREATION STORY

Here is the land upon which the Great Spirit smiled, telling medicine man Spotted Bear and his people that the animals would provide everything they needed if they treated them like brothers. In particular, he instructed them to thank the buffalo and to kill them only if necessary, but the Great Spirit was angered by the needless waste of others who came to this land, fishing and hunting only for sport. Soon all the people were destroying the streams, forests and the buffalo. Angered, the Great Spirit allowed the smoke of their fires to choke them and brought rains upon the land. The people escaped to higher altitudes, but as the rains continued, they were forced to the high peaks, where the medicine man exhorted them to live in peace and return to the way of the buffalo. There they found a white buffalo hide and stretched it above them and across the entire Yellowstone Valley. Spotted Bear stood in the Bridger Mountains and anchored the hide to peaks in all directions. Then he raised one end to allow the West Wind to lift it into a dome to protect the people, the animals and the valley from the devastating rains. As peace was once again restored to the land, the Great Spirit stopped the rains, the sun shone and the white hide gleamed in colors of red, white and blue. As the huge skin shrank, all that remained was a magnificent rainbow arch across the Yellowstone Valley.

CRATER LAKE • TRIUMPH OF
THE ABOVE WORLD

MAKLAK STORY

Almost eight thousand years ago, the Maklaks, known as the people of the marsh, and ancestors of the present-day Klamath Indians, witnessed the eruption of Mount Mazama. This volcanic mountain was the passageway to the Kingdom of Light for the spirit Llal, Chief of the Below World, who lived in the darkness deep inside. One time, Llal left the depths of Mount Mazama and came up onto Earth, where he fell in love with the tribal chief's beautiful daughter and promised her eternal life if she would return with him to his lodge below the mountain. When she refused, he became angry and declared that he would destroy her people with fire. The mighty Chief of the Above World, Skell, took pity on the people and defended them from the top of Mount Shasta. From their mountain tops, the two chiefs waged a furious battle, hurling red-hot rocks as large as hills, causing earth tremors and great landslides of fire. While the people fled in terror to the waters of Klamath Lake, two old medicine men offered to sacrifice themselves and jumped into the pit of fire on top of the mountain. The Chief of the Above World was moved by their bravery and drove Llal back into Mount Mazama. When the sun rose, the great Mount Mazama was gone. It had fallen in on Llal, and all that remained was a large chasm. Torrential rains filled it with the clear water the Maklaks called Lake of Blue Waters, a place where they came to bathe and to receive visions of the inner world of the spirit.

OPPOSITE:
APPROACHING STORM OVER WIZARD ISLAND, CRATER LAKE
NATIONAL PARK, OREGON

Rising majestically near the west shore of the lake is Wizard Island, home of the Spirit Chief who rules over the Land of the Dead. According to tradition, it is here that the ancestors emerged from deep in the earth, through a cave in Crater Lake; deceased spirits are also returned to the lake, with evil ones confined to the fire pit at the top of the cone known as Wizard Island. The Spirit Chief decreed that only wise elders could approach his realm to commune with the ances-tor spirits. Because this island is sacred to the contemporary Klamath Indians, they do not re-veal its Native name.

At 1,932 feet, Oregon's Crater Lake is the deep-est lake in North America, and some say it con-tains the purest water in the world. Although it lies at an altitude of nine thousand feet in the Cascade Range, the water rarely freezes because its large volume acts as a heat reservoir.

"WINGS," SUN REFLECTED IN TIDAL
POOL, LONG BEACH, PACIFIC RIM
NATIONAL PARK, BRITISH COLUMBIA

*The Strait of Juan de Fuca is a long
and narrow channel that separates
Washington's Olympic Peninsula from
Vancouver Island, British Columbia.
This is the land of the Nuu-chah-nulth
(Nootka), with more than a dozen
groups living on the west coast of the
island, and one, the Makah, at the tip
of the peninsula. The name Nootka comes
from nu-tka, meaning "to go around."
When Captain James Cook arrived on the
west coast of Vancouver Island in 1778,
he thought this was part of the mainland. The native Mowachaht people
directed him to explore around the
island, and misunderstanding their
words, he mistakenly gave them this
as a name, which persists to the present.*

STRAIGHT OF JUAN DE FUCA • WATERS OF LIFE

NUU-CHAH-NULTH LORE

Nuu-chah-nulth stories tell of spirit beings and supernatural powers seen all around them, such as the salmon who lives in the house beneath the sea, and Thunderbird, who can beat his wings to make thunder, blink his eyes to cause lightning and pick up a whale as easily as an eagle carries off a trout. Today, these creatures seem to appear silently and unexpectedly in the shape of a gnarled tree root or in the weathered contours of driftwood.

WHALE HUNTING RITUALS

The reputation of the Nuu-chah-nulth as great whalers lives on, although this way of life is now gone. Harpooning the whales from forty-foot dugout canoes was much more than a means of subsistence; it was a religious act of the highest order, a ritual hunt by the select few who had earned the right to take part. For weeks the chief whaler, and later his crew, prepared by bathing in a secret prayer pool as the moon grew to fullness. In order to win the favor of the whale spirits, they did not eat meat or engage in sexual activity, and they rubbed their bodies with hemlock branches to rid themselves of human odors.

According to the Nuu-chah-nulth, women were directly linked to the whale spirit. Prior to the hunt, the wife of the chief whaler would lie on her bed like a docile whale in order to break the bond tying her to the animal. She would stay there until she received word of a successful hunt. Then came a time of great rejoicing. The whole village rushed to the beach to assist, and the women gave thanks to the great whale spirit.

ARBUTUS BARK, VICTORIA,
BRITISH COLUMBIA

"SPIRIT WATERS," WATER REFLECTION IN HARBOR, VICTORIA, BRITISH COLUMBIA

"COSMIC LEAP," COMPOSITE OF HUMPBACK WHALE AND RAINBOW, PACIFIC OCEAN

The Nuu-chah-nulth believe they have lived here forever, and certainly there is evidence of human habitation since the last glacier receded eleven thousand years ago. They moved from ocean-side summer encampments to wintering grounds in more sheltered villages on inland streams, making use of the rich seasonal resources in both the maritime and forest environments. The mighty spruce, hemlock and cedar provided planks for canoes, bent-box containers and totem poles.

NORTH

MORTUARY POLES, NINSTINTS, ANTHONY ISLAND, QUEEN CHARLOTTE ISLANDS, BRITISH COLUMBIA

The 154 islands that make up the Queen Charlottes, located fifty miles west of the British Columbia mainland, are the only part of Canada that escaped the last ice age. To the Haida people, who have thrived here for ten thousand years, they are known as Gwaii Haanas, Islands of Wonder.

Off the southwest coast of the large southern island called Moresby is Anthony Island. Here is the ancient village of Sgan Gwaii, or red cod island town. It is more popularly known as Ninstints, the European version of the word for the village head chief, Nan stins, or "He Who Is Two."

GWAII HAANAS • ISLANDS OF WONDER

HAIDA TRADITION

Now designated a United Nations World Heritage Site, the ancient ceremonial village of Sgan Gwaii in the Gwaii Haanas, or Islands of Wonder, is distinguished by fifteen totem poles carved more than 150 years ago by Haida artists who were revered for their skill. Some are mortuary poles featuring containers for the ashes of the dead. Others, known as frontal posts, identify great lodges; the moon and thunderbird, for example, signal the house of an early chief called Koyah, or Raven, who was the chief servant of Sha-lana, the Creator.

Uninhabited by humans since 1880 when its population was decimated by smallpox, the village today is home to the honored spirits of the dead, and to the ancient carvings that are slowly being returned to the verdant mosses and thousand-year-old trees of the forest. But the Haida of Sgan Gwaii are not forgotten. Their tradition lives on in the work of contemporary artists who are known throughout the world for their exquisite designs in argillite and silver, as well as cedar.

A STREAM INTO FANNY BAY, SOUTH MORESBY, QUEEN CHARLOTTE ISLANDS, BRITISH COLUMBIA

SITKA • HOME OF THE TOTEM SPIRITS

TLINGIT LORE

The coastal rainforests produce straight, tall trees, ideal for totem carvings. One Tlingit story relates how a carved log washed up on the beach, inspiring the people to record their history in cedar and to paint the carved stories with pigments made from hematite, graphite and copper.

The Tlingit universe abounds with spirits; it is said that omens can be heard in the hoot of an owl or the cry of a raven. In this world, the shaman mediates between humans and the kushtakas, the powerful Land Otter People who save those lost in the forest or at sea. Because those saved are then transformed into half-human, half-otter beings like their rescuers, it is the shaman's task to reclaim the lost spirit before the kushtaka can transform it. The stories of these legendary struggles were often recorded on totem poles.

DETAIL OF TOTEM POLE, SITKA NATIONAL HISTORIC PARK, ALASKA

DETAIL OF TOTEM POLE, SITKA
NATIONAL HISTORIC PARK, ALASKA

*Sitka is situated on Tongass Island, which
lies at the northern end of the chain of
islands dotting the southeast coast of
Alaska. Although Sitka takes its name from
Russian fur traders, Tlingit Indian stories
tell how their ancestors migrated here ten
thousand years ago as the glaciers started to
retreat, coming to the temperate coast from
inland homes in the Nass Valley.*

*The Tlingit are also renowned for
their ornamented woven baskets and
Chilkat blankets, which are unique to this
area. Created with fibers from the inner
bark of cedar and mountain goat wool, the
blankets incorporate traditional and semi-
religious motifs designed by men, which are
then woven by women. To achieve the
customarily rich hues and elaborate designs,
the wool used in these highly valued
ceremonial blankets is soaked in dyes made
from black hemlock bark, yellow tree moss
and corroded copper, which produces blue-
green tones.*

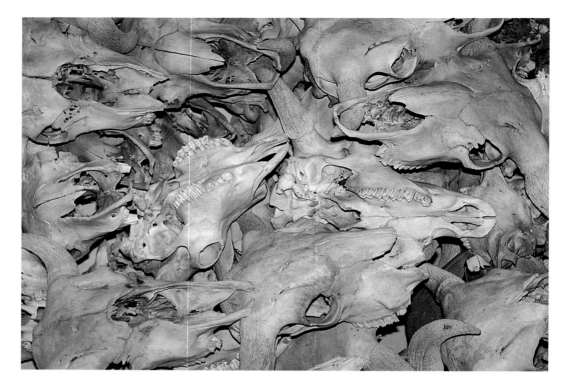

BISON SKULLS, HEAD-SMASHED-IN BUFFALO JUMP, NEAR FORT MAC-CLEOD, ALBERTA

Head-Smashed-In is one of the oldest, largest and best-preserved buffalo jumps in North America. Located near present-day Fort Macleod, Alberta, where prairies and mountains meet, the thirty-three-foot cliff was used for hunts as early as 3700 B.C. The Blackfoot Nation, or Nitsitapii (meaning "real people"), believe they are the only ones to have made use of this jump, which was traditionally called Piskun.

HEAD-SMASHED-IN • CLIMAX OF THE HUNT

BLACKFOOT HUNTING RITUALS

The name Head-Smashed-In comes from the Peigan tribe of the Blackfoot, from a story told about a young man who was mortally wounded as he hid below the overhang to watch the buffalo fall.

Prehunt rituals of dances and songs included prayers to call the buffalo, using a sacred Buffalo Stone called the Iniskim. Buffalo runners, who disguised themselves as animals and lured the buffalo over the cliff, fasted for days prior to the jump and prayed to the Great Buffalo Spirit to deliver a bountiful hunt; they also smudged themselves with sacred sweetgrass, and chewed it to increase their endurance. As many as five hundred people worked together, without the benefit of horses, to herd the buffalo and channel them into a drive lane. Buffalo that survived the impact of the jump were killed by hunters at the bottom to prevent them from warning other herds about the trap.

"PROPHECY," SILHOUETTES OF BISON, UNIDENTIFIED PRAIRIE

Within view of Head-Smashed-In is Chief Mountain, revered by a number of tribes in the region. Called Ukimazi by the Cree, and Ninaistuki by the Blackfoot, Chief Mountain is known as the home of the Wind Spirit and Thunderbird. A young man, seeking his life-guiding animal spirit in a vision quest, often chooses a site where he can view sacred forms such as Chief Mountain, Crows Nest Mountain, or the Sweetgrass Hills. This helps assure communion with the Great Spirit. Traditionally, the vision seeker tied a buffalo skull to thongs attached to skewers that pierced the skin on his chest and dragged the skull up the mountain.

SNOW PATTERN AND REFLECTION ON SLOPE AT SENTINEL PASS, LARCH VALLEY, ROCKY
MOUNTAINS, BANFF NATIONAL PARK, ALBERTA

*On the steep scree slopes of Larch Valley, overlooking the Valley of the Ten Peaks
in Banff National Park, the trail snakes around Sentinel Mountain (called
Nitai-istuki, or Lone Mountain, by the Blackfoot), affording a commanding
view before it descends into Paradise Valley. At these high points, concave
"prayer seats" or "fasting beds" fashioned out of rock show where a young man
would seek to make contact with the spirits during a vision quest.*

SHINING MOUNTAINS • BACKBONE OF THE WORLD

BLACKFOOT LORE

The earliest written historical records in the 1760s refer to Indian reports about the "mountains of crystals" in the far west. The Blackfoot (Nitsitapii) translated this to Mistukiz-Ikanaziaw, but also call the Rocky Mountains the "Backbone of the World," and know this range as the home of spirit powers that include Wind Maker, Cold Maker and Thunder. They believe the Great Spirit is everywhere—in the waters, trees, birds and animals, as well as the mountains and sky. Natos, the Sun, is the creative power who is the source of life; he provides for the people as long as they revere all nature, and he warms the land that is filled with his presence.

THE STORY OF STAR BOY

The power of Natos is seen in the traditional Blackfoot story of Poia (Scarface), or Star Boy, who lived in the sky. He and his mother, Feather Woman, were banished to the Earth for digging up a sacred turnip. She dies of grief, leaving Star Boy alone. The object of a great deal of ridicule because of the scar on his face, Star Boy journeys to the mountains in search of Natos, following the path of the Sun to the Sun's lodge. Natos removes Star Boy's scar and appoints him his messenger. He is to tell the Blackfoot that Natos will cure their sickness if they give a Sundance every year. So Star Boy learns the Sundance songs and prayers and returns to instruct the people. According to the Blackfoot, each step of Star Boy's sacred journey can be seen today in the mountains and hills of their nation.

NA'PI, THE KEEPER OF MEN

Where the foothills meet the mountains, one can see Na'pi, the Keeper of Men, who rejected the Chief Woman because she was poorly dressed. When she reappeared in her finery, Na'pi chose her as his wife. She refused, and in retaliation turned him into a lone pine tree. The beautiful setting where this took place is a reminder that appearances can deceive.

ST. ELIAS • FATHER OF THE PEAKS

TLINGIT LEGEND

The Yakutat tribe of the Coastal Tlingit culture speaks of a time when all the world was covered in a deluge, with only the peaks of Mount St. Elias and two other summits to guide the ancestors and give them refuge on their journey from the north. The Tlingit have a traditional song that honors Mount St. Elias for opening the world with sunshine and bringing great happiness to the people.

Another Tlingit story recalls when Mount St. Elias married Mount Fairweather, visible today one hundred miles to the east. It was a turbulent relationship, resulting in Mount St. Elias moving west, leaving a trail of peaks in between as slaves to mark the way, and retaining one slave as a go-between. The mountains to the east are identified as their children, who stayed with Fairweather, their mother.

Because the Tlingit believe that spirits inhabit mountains and glaciers, only shamans seeking supernatural powers would climb up to the higher slopes. The rest of the tribe were careful not to offend the spirits, addressing these landforms with respect by wearing proper dress, avoiding eye contact and covering their faces with pitch so as not to appear to be staring at the mountains. Retreating glaciers, with moraines that resemble long braided hair, are believed to be female, while male glaciers are considered more dangerous and more easily provoked to anger. Many attendant taboos were put into effect to prevent disasters. Several glaciers along the flanks of Mount St. Elias are said to harbor mysterious but harmless spirits that look like giant worms.

OPPOSITE:
APPROACHING STORM, UNIDENTIFIED MOUNTAIN PASS, ST. ELIAS MOUNTAINS, YUKON

Mount St. Elias, which lies in the southwest corner of the Yukon bordering Alaska, is part of the Canadian Cordillera, which includes nearby Mount Logan, the highest point in Canada. Two hundred years ago, this region was in the last stages of a minor ice age in which a series of valley glaciers descended from the heights of Mount St. Elias, through the Alsek Pass and into the sea in Yakutat Bay.

SHISHMAREF • PLACE OF THE GREAT WHALE SPIRIT

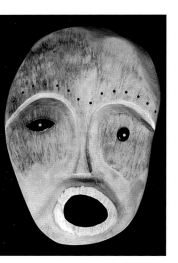

INUPIAT TRADITION

The tradition of mask carving among the Inupiat people is a religious art, learned from and practiced on behalf of the spirits by the shaman. Carving a mask enabled a shaman to intercede in the interest of his people and maintain harmony and balance with the spirit embodied in the mask. The spirit in the mask is thought to contain the vital force of not only the animal depicted but the whole chain of individual spirits of that genus.

Using large, open boats called umiaks, made from the skins of bearded seals, the traditional Inupiat community hunted whales and other large marine mammals. Preparatory feasts were held before the spring hunt; at this festival of renewal, all remaining whale meat from the previous year was distributed to indicate that only what was required would be taken, and to demonstrate to the whale that the village was worthy of the hunt. To ensure that spirit forms of the whale would be regenerated, special rituals included offering the whale a drink of water and opening a skull to release its spirit.

LEFT:
INUPIAT WHALE BONE MASK CARVED BY EDWIN J. WEYIOUANNA, SHISHMAREF, ALASKA

OPPOSITE:
"NIGHT MYSTERY," WET SAND AND SUNLIGHT ON WATER, MENDENHALL GLACIER, JUNEAU, ALASKA

The Inupiat village of Shishmaref lies just below the Arctic Circle on the Bering Strait, which divides Alaska and Russia. The peninsula on which it sits is believed to be a remnant of the ancient land bridge called Beringia, which allowed early Asian people to journey to North America.

CAVE OF THE ELDERS, PICTOGRAPH CAVES STATE PARK, MONTANA

PICTOGRAPH CAVE • AMPHITHEATER OF MYSTERY

At Pictograph Caves State Park near Billings, Montana, there are three caves tucked high
into the steep sandstone cliff that forms a large amphitheater exposed to the southwest.
Originally carved by the meanderings of the Yellowstone River, they were further enlarged
by wind erosion and moisture seepage.

 Of these three caves, Pictograph is by far the largest. Its walls display a blend of mineral stains and red ocher images of animals, birds and human figures painted some fifteen
hundred years ago. At the western end of the cliff is a grotto called Ghost Cave, so named
because the remains of three early inhabitants were found here around 1940. The mar-
velously sculpted wall of the middle cave, aptly known as the Cave of the Elders, was
formed over millions of years by the hardening of mineral compounds left by ocean
plants and shellfish when this area was covered by a primordial sea.

BADLANDS • VALLEY OF THE SPIRITS

BLACKFOOT LEGEND
The Blackfoot identify this as the place where the first Buffalo Stone was found more than one thousand years ago. These ammonite and baculite fossils, known as Iniskim, carry the animate power of the bull and are part of the sacred bundle used in the Buffalo Calling Ceremony. They are a source of personal sacred power that can appear in human form or in a dream and are used in other ceremonies such as planting the sacred tobacco garden.

SHOSHONE PETROGLYPHS
The hoodoo formations and rock carvings along the Milk River are special places for the Shoshone and Blackfoot. It is said that they mirror the spirit presence. Some archaeologists believe the petroglyphs were made by the Shoshone Tribe, ancestors of the Great Basin people. Blackfoot or Nitsitapii traditions, on the other hand, tell us that the markings such as those at Writing-on-Stone (called Masinasin by the Cree) were created by the spirits.

RIGHT:
EROSIONAL MARKINGS ON SAND-
STONE, DINOSAUR PROVINCIAL PARK,
BROOKS, ALBERTA

*The southern edge of the badlands
includes high sandstone cliffs and
enigmatic rock formations that seem
to echo and moan with the wind.*

OPPOSITE:
HOODOOS, RED DEER RIVER VALLEY,
DRUMHELLER, ALBERTA

*The recent history of the badlands is not
well known. Most of our knowledge is
focused on the period 65 million years ago
when the region was a swamp inhabited by
flesh-eating tyrannosaurs and plant-eating
hadrosaurs. Canada's largest tract of badlands stretches south from Drumheller,
Alberta, to the Montana border. The area
between Dinosaur Provincial Park and
Brooks contains one of the world's richest
fossil beds making the soil ideal for the
sacred sagebrush, whose greenery is burned
to smudge or purify.*

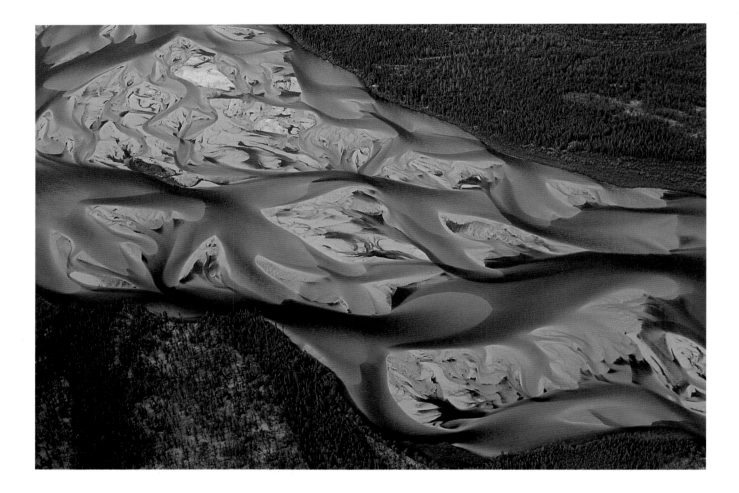

WILLIAM RIVER • BRAIDS OF FANTASY

CHIPEWYAN ORIGIN STORY

Eight thousand years ago, the Paleo-Indians followed the caribou migrations from their summer range on the open tundra into this winter range in the boreal forest. More recently, the two-thousand-year-old Taltheilei culture were forebears to the ancestors of the present-day Chipewyan tribe of the Dene Nation. The Chipewyan origin story tells of the union of Primeval Woman with a dog that was transformed into a man at night.

DENE NATION LORE

Many Dene traditions deal with the relationship between humans and nature, including the belief that spirit-animal beings enter dreams, giving humans power to control the migration of game and other natural phenomena. One Dene story tells of how Hottah, the moose, directs a young man named Caribou-Footed to help the chief of the Sky Country find his stolen medicine belt. The Northern Lights are messages from him, telling his brothers on Earth about the great home beyond the sky.

OPPOSITE:
AERIAL VIEW OF BOTTOM SAND PATTERNS, WILLIAM RIVER, ATHABASCA SAND DUNES
PARK LAND RESERVE, SASKATCHEWAN

Located at the edge of the boreal forest in northern Saskatchewan, the waters of Lake Athabasca eventually drain into the Beaufort Sea in the western Arctic. The world's largest sand dunes at this latitude are here, formed more than ten thousand years ago and continuously in motion for the past six thousand years. Here the William River carves its way northward through the Athabasca Sand Dunes, carrying millions of tons of sand and emptying them into a broad V-shaped delta on the southern shore of Lake Athabasca. From the air, the patterns created by the river's flow seem magical; the sandy bottom is visible through the pure, clear current, the deepest sections revealing the darker shapes and the shallower areas creating the brighter tones.

CAMERA MOTION ON POPLAR GROVE IN SUNSET LIGHT, GREAT SANDHILLS, SASKATCHEWAN

THE GREAT SANDHILLS • PLACE OF THE LITTLE PEOPLE

CREE "LITTLE PEOPLE"

This fragile environment shelters a rare and diverse selection of native grasses and protects the Memekweciwak, the "little people" of Plains Cree oral history. These dwarfs, who are responsible for making chipped-flint arrowheads, live in sandy riverbanks and sandhills. They can grant powers and are highly desired as spirit guides.

The Nitsitapii or Blackfoot people also believe the spirits of their ancestors reside here in the Great Sandhills.

DAWN LIGHT ON SAND RIDGE, GREAT SANDHILLS, SASKATCHEWAN

The Great Sandhills in southwest Saskatchewan are a 300,000-acre post-glacial desert surrounded by prairie. This unique island of sand encloses some stable dunes that rise several hundred feet, as well as others that constantly shift in the wind, removing the tracks of mule deer, antelope and rabbits that take refuge here.

WANUSKEWIN · VALLEY OF PEACE

An hour's walk through this valley leads to two buffalo jumps, numerous tipi rings, a medicine wheel and nineteen archaeological sites that attest to more than six thousand years of habitation by the Plains Indians. Today, Wanuskewin continues to be used for sweat lodge ceremonies. Wes Fineday, a Cree guide at Wanuskewin, says that although all the earth is sacred, this valley is a special place, a haven of neutrality where tribes laid down their arms. Wanuskewin draws people to learn, to partake in ceremony, to fast and to attain help from spirit powers.

According to Fineday, Wanuskewin is one of many extraordinary places where it is possible to achieve an understanding of one's position in the world. This understanding requires going to a place of knowledge deep inside, and leads to a sense of harmony that allows one to form a connection with the "land beyond the mist . . . the land in the memory." Fineday hopes that visitors here will be touched by the essence and start to know their own spirit, fulfilling the invitation of Wanuskewin to "see nature like an eagle."

The valley that opens onto the South Saskatchewan River just three miles north of Saskatoon is named Wanuskewin, Cree for "seeking peace of mind" or "living in harmony." The name Saskatoon comes from Mis-sask-quah-too-min, the Cree word meaning "red willow berry." Not only does this tranquil valley provide a spiritual retreat for those seeking peace of mind, but it also stands as a magnificent example of harmony among people. Five Indian Nations, three levels of government and local corporations cooperated in the development and protection of this area as a heritage site.

FIRST SNOWFALL OF THE SEASON, WANUSKEWIN HERITAGE PARK, SASKATOON, SASKATCHEWAN

"WHITE CANOE," DETAIL OF
BEACHED ICEBERG, ESKIMO POINT,
MANITOBA

*Inuit settlements on the west coast of
Hudson Bay date back at least four
thousand years. Eskimo Point, near
Churchill, Manitoba, is a twentieth-
century village, but Eskimo Point in the
Northwest Territories has been an Inuit
summer camp for more than five hundred years. It has recently reverted to its
original name, Arviat, meaning "place
of the bowhead whale."*

DETAIL OF BEACHED ICEBERG, ESKIMO POINT, MANITOBA

ESKIMO POINT • LAND OF THE INUIT

INUIT TRADITION

The Inuit have traditionally constructed figures of rock on the vast expanses of tundra.
These structures are called inukshuks, meaning "acting in the capacity of a human."
They function as the visual language of the people, serving as personal message centers to
hunters, as "caribou drives" or "drift fences" to guide game, and even as indicators to
kayakers in sight of land. Some are revered as locations of power, never to be touched or
approached. Others are believed to bring good fortune and are venerated and given gifts.
Perhaps the best way to describe the significance of these landmarks is in the words of an
Inuit hunter who, pointing to one, said, "This attaches me to my ancestors and to the
land." In English we have no word for the Inuit "unganaqtuq nyna," meaning a deep and
total attachment to the earth.

MOOSE MOUNTAIN • CIRCLE WITHOUT END

At the summit of a 560-foot treeless hill called Moose Mountain, in southeast Saskatchewan, lies a medicine wheel with five lines of stones radiating from a central cairn. In this area dominated by plains, the mountainous setting is unusual, overlooking lush undulating hills rolling down to the relatively flat prairie landscape in the distance. A multitude of tipi rings in the area indicates that for untold generations this was the home of Cree and Assiniboine encampments that thrived on the bounty of the game and the shelter provided by nearby groves. The wheel is located on land that is now privately owned, and is protected by the Cree family which lives here.

No one really knows why or when this medicine wheel was built. Archaeologists who have studied the eighty major medicine wheels in North America—of which nearly sixty are found in the Canadian Prairies—suggest this one may have been used for animal divination; others believe it portrays astronomical alignments that could have been seen either two thousand years ago or three hundred years ago. Some current opinions dispute this theory because the nomadic hunting cultures of the Plains Indians did not follow the stars, and their stories do not contain astronomical themes. It is known that Plains Indian people named prominent hills, using their features for navigation, and that stone cairns found on outlying hills appear to align with the spokes of this wheel. One investigator has compared these to inukshuks (stone cairns) of the Arctic, which were used as message centers and directional aids for travel in the tundra.

VIEW FROM SUMMIT, SUNSET LIGHT, MOOSE MOUNTAIN MEDICINE WHEEL, SASKATCHEWAN

JOURNEY'S END

The Moose Mountain Medicine Wheel is the culmination of our journey, a final stone in the circular path we have followed around North America. The round symbol speaks of infinity and of continuity in life; everything in the natural world operates in cycles that are repeated over and over, giving us the opportunity to enter into this never-ending path. The circle also speaks of the interconnectedness of all things, the equality of all life, and suggests that by living in harmony with the world around us, we too can experience a deep and abiding peace.

Still others suggest this wheel is a good example of a Thirst Dance site, the annual Cree ceremony similar to the Sundance, which was often held in the hills to pray for rains to nourish grasslands and buffalo. Perhaps the most important explanation comes from Cree elders who say that medicine wheels belong to another creation time; they were made for ceremonies by their ancestors and are sacred grounds that should not be disturbed.

"FULL CIRCLE," CENTRAL CAIRN, MOOSE MOUNTAIN MEDICINE WHEEL, SASKATCHEWAN

PHOTOGRAPHER'S NOTES

My journey to the twenty-eight spokes of the medicine wheel did not occur in the order in which they are presented here. My visits to the many locations began with a 1971 hike over Sentinal Pass in Banff National Park (see Shining Mountains, p. 103) and ended with an exploration of the Rock Eagle Effigy near Atlanta, Georgia in October of 1993 (p. 36), just prior to the completion of this book. Much of my travel was by Volkswagen camper (1961, 1966, 1972 and 1986 models successively), which provided not only transportation but also an office, equipment storage space, library, kitchen and sleeping quarters. I like to think of these excursions as borrowing from the lifestyle of the turtle: although the pace was relatively slow, particularly during uphill hauls and stretches into the wind, I carried my house with me, and thus could camp in remote locations, ready for an early morning shoot. Other modes of conveyance included a cruise ship, a hot air balloon, a motorized rubber raft, a canoe, small aircraft, a 4-wheel drive jeep, kayaks, a train and numerous motorboats and rental cars.

I work exclusively with 35mm color slides, and these were made with a variety of brands: Ektachrome, Kodachrome, Fujichrome, Fujichrome Velvia and Agfachrome. My choice of film is determined by the effect I wish to achieve, the quality of light, the time of day and the desired color intensity. Generally I shoot Kodachrome in low contrast light and when subtlety or a pastel effect is called for; Ektachrome when a greater latitude of tones is present in the scene; Fujichrome for brilliance and for the greatest variation of nature's green tones; Fujichrome Velvia for the ultimate in color saturation and sharpness; and Agfachrome for rustic portrayal of earth tones.

For camera stability and precise composition, I use a Manfrotto model 055 tripod (marketed as Bogan in the United States), and either an Amplis or Manfrotto ball and socket head, for virtually all my work. The 35mm format is ideal for portability of camera, film and lenses—a crucial consideration when photographing in remote locales—and allows for convenient storage of mounted slides. By 1985 I was using eighteen lenses ranging from an 8mm fisheye to a 4200mm telephoto, but my workhorse lens has been my Nikkor 80-200mm f2.8 zoom. I rarely use filters but occasionally add a polarizer for added definition, or a color enhancer to give emphasis to warmer tones.

On long trips I carry several camera bodies, my favorite being the Nikon F3, which I usually leave on the automatic exposure mode, manipulating the manual override as required. I often work with two cameras so that a second one is ready immediately after I finish a roll of film. Sometimes I load each camera with different film so I can compare the results or achieve a contrasting effect.

As a general rule, I organized my time so that I was on location before dawn, relaxing during the midday light, then returning for more photography an hour or two prior to sunset. Often I continued photographing into the night, sometimes lighting my foregrounds artificially or using long exposure times for special results. My favorite example of the multiple flash technique is "Lunar Necklace" (p. 59). Casa Rinconada is a large circular stone structure, its roof open to the sky. I obtained special permission to be there after dark. Prior to the rising of the full moon, I set my camera in the center with a fisheye lens (180° angle of view) pointing straight up and focused on infinity, the stone perimeter showing in the viewfinder as a complete circle. Then at a distance of a few feet inside the wall, I circled the structure, lighting the wall with about twenty-five equidistant flashes, finishing with a strobe into each of the thirty-five portals before ending the exposure. Then I waited twenty minutes for the full moon to rise above the east wall, and made a second exposure on the same frame. Every fifteen minutes thereafter, I tripped the shutter, thus tracing the orbit of the moon across the sky. A sleeping bag, lawn chair and alarm clock allowed me to doze in comfort between exposures.

The circular image of the Moose Mountain Medicine Wheel (p. 122) was also made with a fisheye lens. In this case I stood over the central cairn, pointing the camera downwards so that the complete horizon, as well as my feet and legs, were visible in the viewfinder. Later I worked with the photo lab to electronically remove the feet and legs from the image and to extend the blue sky in every direction. Computer technology was also used to combine parts of three photographs to achieve the effect of the moon rising over the human effigy at Manito Ahbee (p. 15).

Sometimes I find that special effects allow me to convey the essence of a site more readily than would a documentary image, and I have identified composites and multiple or long exposures in the picture captions. But the vast majority of my photographs are straightforward images that need no manipulation to convey the spirit of the place.

This book is a collection of images expressing my personal responses to these sacred landscapes, rather than an attempt to portray in some objective way what a visitor might see. I made about a thousand photographs per site—sometimes two or three thousand—knowing that on the average only one or two images would be selected for the book. Choosing the photographs involved several waves of "honing down," as I worked in a team that included the editor, book designer and researcher. We always asked first whether the photograph caught the spirit of the place, and second whether it worked with the overall flow of the book.

Because the images I made and the images we chose are an expression of my own way of seeing, the creation of this book has been a deeply personal experience. Perhaps the greatest lessons for a photographer are not in learning to master camera technique, but in learning the true meaning of humility and how to dance in a spirit of cooperation.

REFERENCES

Allen, D. *Totem Poles of the Northwest*. Surrey, British Columbia: Hancock House Publishers, 1977.

Allen, Paula Gunn. *The Sacred Hoop, Recovering the Feminine in American Indian Traditions*. Boston: Beacon Press, 1986.

Angel, Myron. *The Painted Rock of California, A Legend (1910)*. San Luis Obispo, California: Padre Productions, 1979.

Anishnaabe Kinoomagewin, Curriculum Development. *Espanola*. Ontario: Anishnabe Spiritual Center, 1992.

Ashwell, Reg. *Indian Tribes of the Northwest*. Surrey, British Columbia: Hancock House Publishers, 1977.

Atkinson, Richard. *White Sands, Wind, Sand and Time*. Tucson: Southwest Parks and Monuments Association, 1977.

Beck, Mary Giraudo. *Shamans and Kushtakas, North Coast Tales of the Supernatural*. Bothell, Washington: Alaska Northwest Books, 1991.

Beck, Peggy V., Anna Lee Walters, and Nia Francisco. *The Sacred, Ways of Knowledge, Sources of Life*. Tsaile, Arizona: Navajo Community College Press, 1990.

Benzinger, Charles. *Chaco Journey: Remembrance and Awakening*. Sante Fe: Timewindow Publications, 1988.

Berenholtz, Jim. *Journey to the Four Directions*. Sante Fe: Bear & Co, 1993.

Bernbaum, Edwin. *Sacred Mountains of the World*. San Francisco: Sierra Club, 1990.

Berry, Thomas. *The Dream of the Earth*. San Francisco: Sierra Club, 1988.

Bierhorst, John. *The Mythology of North America*. New York: William Morrow and Co., 1985.

Bierhorst, John, ed. *The Sacred Path: Spells, Prayers and Power Songs of the American Indians*. New York: Quill, 1984.

Blackburn, Thomas C. *December's Child, A Book of Chumash Oral Narratives*. Berkeley: University of California Press, 1975.

Black Elk, Wallace, and William S. Lyon. *Black Elk, The Sacred Ways of a Lakota*. New York: HarperCollins, 1990.

Brace, Ian. "Boulder Monuments of Saskatchewan." Masters Thesis, University of Alberta, Edmonton, 1987.

Brown, Joseph Epes, ed. *The Sacred Pipe, Black Elk's Account of the Seven Rites of the Oglala Sioux*. Norman, Oklahoma: University of Oklahoma Press, 1953.

Brown, Joseph Epes. *The Spiritual Legacy of the American Indian*. New York: Crossroad Publishing, 1992.

Brown, Vinson. *Voices of Earth and Sky*. Happy Camp, California: Naturegraph, 1974.

Bruchac, Joseph, and Diana Landau. *Singing of Earth, A Native American Anthology*. Berkeley: The Nature Company, 1993.

Buffalo Hunters, The. Alexandria: Time Life, 1993.

Burger, Julian. *The Gaia Atlas of First Peoples: A Future for the Indigenous World*. New York: Anchor Books/ Doubleday, 1990.

Burland, Cottie, Irene Nicholson, and Harold Osborne. *Mythology of the Americas*. London: Hamlyn, 1975.

Buswa, Ernestine, and Jean Shawana, eds. *Teachings of the Medicine Wheel (Nishnaabe Bimaadziwin Kinoomaadwinan)*. West Bay, Ontario: Ojibwe Cultural Foundation, 1992.

Caduto, Michael J., and Joseph Bruchac. Keepers of the Earth: Native Stories and Environmental Activities for Children. Saskatoon, Saskatchewan: Fifth House Publishers, 1989.

Caldwell, Joseph R., and Robert Hall, eds. Hopewellian Studies. Scientific Papers, Vol. XII, Illinois State Museum, Springfield, 1977.

Campbell, Elizabeth W. Crozer. *An Archeological Survey of the Twenty Nine Palms Region*. Los Angeles: Southwest Museum Papers Number Seven, 1931, 1963.

Campbell, Joseph. *The Inner Reaches of Outer Space: Metaphor as Myth and as Religion*. New York: Harper and Row, 1986.

Campbell, Joseph. *The Mythic Image*. Princeton: Princeton University Press, 1974.

Cantor, George. *North American Indian Landmarks, A Traveller's Guide*. Detroit: Visible Ink Press 1993.

Carter, Anthony. *This is Haida*. Vancouver, British Columbia: Agency Press Ltd., 1968.

Charging Eagle, Tom, and Ron Zeilinger. *Black Hills: Sacred Hills*. Chamberlain, South Dakota: Tipi Press, 1987.

Chetwynd, Tom. *Dictionary of Sacred Myth*. Unwin Paperbacks, 1986.

Clark, Ella Elizabeth. *Indian Legends of Canada*. Toronto: McClelland and Stewart, 1960, 1983.

Coe, Michael, Dean Snow, and Elizabeth Benson. *Atlas of Ancient America*. New York: Facts on File, 1986.

Complete Guide to America's National Parks. Washington, D.C.: National Park Foundation, 1992–1993.

Corbett, Cynthia. *Power Trips: Journey to Sacred Sites as a Way of Transformation*. Santa Fe: Timewindow Publications, 1988.

Cotta Vaz, Mark. *Spirit in the Land*. New York: Signet Paperback, 1988.

Cornett, James W. *Desert Palm Oasis*. Palm Springs Desert Museum, 1989.

Crawford, J. L. *Zion National Park, Towers of Stone*. Santa Barbara: Sequoia Communications, 1988.

Damas, David, ed. *Handbook of North American Indians, Vol. 5, Arctic*. Washington, DC: Smithsonian, 1984.

Davis, Wade. *Shadows in the Sun, Essays on the Spirit of Place*. Edmonton, Alberta: Lone Pine Publishing, 1992.

Debassige, Blake, and Stephen Hogbin, curators. *Political Landscapes #Two: Sacred and Secular Sites*. Owen Sound, Ontario: Tom Thomson Memorial Art Gallery, 1991.

Douglas, Marjory Stoneman. *The Everglades: River of Grass*. Georgia: Mockingbird Books, 1974, 1984.

Dragoo, Don W. *Mounds for the Dead*. Pittsburgh: Carnegie Museum of Natural History, 1963.

Edmonds, Margot, and Ella E. Clark. *Voices of the Winds, Native American Legends*. New York: Facts on File, 1989.

Erdoes, Richard, and Alfonson Ortiz, eds. *American Indian Myths and Legends*. New York: Pantheon Books, 1984.

European Challenge, The. Alexandria: Time Life, 1992.

Everhart, Ronald E. *Glen Canyon–Lake Powell: The Story Behind the Scenery*. Las Vegas: K. C. Publications, 1983.

Fell, Barry. *America B.C.* New York: Pocket Books, Simon and Schuster, 1976, 1989.

Fidler, J. Havelock. *Earth Energy: A Dowser's Investigation of Ley Lines*. Wellingborough, England: Aquarian Press, 1983, 1988.

First Americans, The. Alexandria, Virginia: Time Life, 1992.

Fortney, David L. *Mysterious Places—Ancient Sites and Lost Cultures*. New York: Random House/Crescent Books, 1992.

Fox, Matthew. *The Coming of the Cosmic Christ*. San Francisco: Harper and Row, 1988.

Frick, Thomas, ed. *Sacred Theory of the Earth*. Berkeley: North Atlantic Books, 1986.

Furst, Peter T. "Roots and Continuities of Shamanism," in *Stones, Bones & Skin: Ritual and Shamanic Art*. Toronto:

artscanada, Dec. 1973-Jan. 1974.

Garfield, Viola E., and Linn A. Forrest. *The Wolf and the Raven, Totem Poles of Southeastern Alaska.* Seattle: University of Washington Press, 1948, 1961–93.

George, Chief Dan. *My Spirit Soars.* Surrey, British Columbia: Hancock House Publishers, 1982.

Golia, Jack de. *Everglades: The Story Behind the Scenery.* Las Vegas: K. C. Publications, 1978.

Gonzales, Magda Weck (Star-Spider Woman), and J. A. Gonzales (Rattling Bar). *Star-Spider Speaks: The Teachings of the Native American Tarot.* Stamford: U.S. Games, Inc., 1990.

Grande, John K. *Art and Environment.* Toronto: The Friendly Chameleon, 1993.

Grant, Campbell. *Rock Art of the American Indian.* Dillon, Colorado: Vistabooks, 1992.

Halifax, Joan. Shaman, *The Wounded Healer.* London: Thames and Hudson, 1982.

Halpin, Marjorie M. *Totem Poles: An Illustrated Guide.* Vancouver, British Columbia: University of British Columbia Press, 1981.

Hallendy, Norman. "Places of Power and Objects of Veneration in the Canadian Arctic." Manuscript, presented to the World Archaelogical Congress, Venezuela, 1990.

Hamilton, Virginia, and Barry Moses. *In the Beginning.* Orlando: Harcourt Brace Jovanovich, 1988.

Harpur, James, and Jennifer Westwood. *The Atlas of Legendary Places.* New York: Weidenfeld and Nicolson, 1989.

Helm, Jane, ed. *Handbook of North American Indians, Vol. 6, Subarctic.* Washington, DC: Smithsonian, 1987.

Hillerman, Tony. *Indian Country, America's Sacred Land.* Weston, Massachusettes: Yearout Editions, 1987.

Hillerman, Tony. *Talking God.* New York: HarperCollins, 1989.

Holsinger, Rosemary, and P. I. Piemme. *Shasta Indian Tales.* Happy Camp, California: Naturegraph Publishers, 1982.

Hudson, Travis. *Guide to Painted Cave.* Santa Barbara: McNally & Loftin, 1982.

Hungry Wolf, Adolph. *A Good Medicine Collection, Life in Harmony with Nature.* Summertown, Tennessee: Book Publishing Co., 1990.

Jackson, Victor L. *Zion: The Continuing Story in Pictures.* Las Vegas: K. C. Publications, 1989.

Jilek, Wolfgang. *Indian Healing: Shamanic Ceremonialism in the Pacific Northwest Today.* Surrey, British Columbia: Hancock House Publishers, 1982.

Jonker, Peter, ed. *Saskatchewan's Endangered Spaces.*

Saskatoon, Saskatchewan: Extension Dept., University of Saskatchewan, 1992.

Joseph, Frank, ed. *Sacred Sites, A Guidebook to Sacred Centers and Mysterious Places in the United States.* St. Paul: Lewellyn Publications, 1992.

Kelemen, Pal. *Art of the Americas: Ancient and Hispanic.* New York: Thomas Crowell, 1969.

Kew, Della, and P. E. Goddard. *Indian Art and Culture of The Northwest Coast.* Surrey, British Columbia: Hancock House Publishers, 1974.

Lame Deer, John (Fire), and Richard Erdoes. *Lame Deer, Seeker of Visions.* New York: Washington Square Press, 1972.

Langdon, Steve J. *The Native People of Alaska.* Anchorage: Greatland Graphics, 1993.

Lankford, George E., ed. *Native American Legends.* Little Rock: August House, 1987.

Leeming, David Adams. *The World of Myth.* New York: Oxford University Press, 1990.

Lehrman, Fredric. *The Sacred Landscape.* Berkeley: Celestial Arts Publishing, 1988.

Leonard, George. *The Silent Pulse.* New York: E.P. Dutton, 1986.

Lister, Robert H. and Florence C. *Those Who Came Before.* Globe, Arizona: Southwest Parks and Monuments, 1983.

Lombardi, Frances G. and Gerald Scott. *Circle Without End.* London: Thames and Hudson, 1979.

Lopez, Barry. *Arctic Dreams: Imagination and Desire in a Northern Landscape.* New York: Charles Scribner's Sons, 1986.

Lopez, Barry. *Crossing Open Ground.* London, England: Pan Books, 1989.

Lothson, Gordon Allan. *The Jeffers Petroglyphs Site, A Survey and Analysis of the Carvings.* St. Paul: Minnesota Historical Society, 1976.

Lowie, Robert H. *Indians of the Plains.* Lincoln, Nebraska: University of Nebraska Press, 1982.

Maclagan, David. Creation Myths: *Man's Introduction to the World.* London: Thames and Hudson, 1977.

Mails, Thomas E. *Secret Native American Pathways, A Guide to Inner Peace.* Tulsa: Council Oak Books, 1988.

Mails, Thomas E. *Fools Crow.* Lincoln, Nebraska: University of Nebraska Press, 1979.

Mails, Thomas E. *The Mystic Warriors of the Plains.* New York: Mallard Press, 1972, 1991.

Mander, Jerry. *In the Absence of the Sacred; The Failure of Technology and the Survival of the Indian Nations.* San Francisco: Sierra Club, 1991.

Manitopyes, Alvin, and Dave Courchene Jr. *Voice of the*

Eagle. Calgary, Alberta: Aboriginal Awareness Society, 1992.

Mann, Nicholas. Sedona, *Sacred Earth.* Prescott, Arizona: Zivah Publishers, 1991.

Marriott, Alice, and Carol Rachlin. *Plains Indian Mythology.* New York: New American Library, 1975.

Matlock, Gary, and Warren Scott. *Enemy Ancestors—The Anasazi World with a Guide to Sites.* Northland Press, 1988.

Maud, Ralph. *A Guide to B.C. Indian Myth and Legend.* Vancouver, British Columbia: Talon Books, 1982.

Maybury-Lewis, David. *Millennium—Tribal Wisdom and the Modern World.* New York: Viking Penguin, 1992.

McCall, Lynne, and Rosalind Perry. *California's Chumash Indians.* Santa Barbara Museum of Natural History, 1986.

McClellan, Catherine. *Part of the Land, Part of the Water: A History of the Yukon Indians.* Vancouver, British Columbia: Douglas and McIntyre, 1987.

McDonald, George F. *Ninstints: Haida World Heritage Site.* Vancouver, British Columbia: University of British Columbia Press, 1983.

McGaa, Ed, *Eagle Man. Mother Earth Spirituality, Native American Paths to Healing Ourselves and Our World.* San Francisco: HarperCollins, 1989, 1990.

McGaa, Ed, *Eagle Man. Rainbow Tribe, Ordinary People Journeying on the Red Road.* San Francisco: HarperCollins, 1992.

McGhee, Robert. *Ancient Canada.* Ottawa, Ontario: Canadian Museum of Civilization, 1989.

Merz, Blanche. *Points of Cosmic Energy.* Essex, England: C.W. Daniel Co. Ltd, 1987.

Michell, John. *The Earth Spirit: Its Ways, Shrines and Mysteries.* London: Thames and Hudson, 1975.

Melville, J. McKim, and Claudia Putnam. *Prehistoric Astronomy in the Southwest.* Boulder: Johnson Books, 1989.

Mighty Chieftains, The. Alexandria: Time Life, 1993.

Miller, Jay. *Earthmaker, Tribal Stories from Native North America.* New York: Perigee Books, 1992.

Miller, Sherrill. *The Pilgrim's Guide to The Sacred Earth.* Distributed by Penguin Books, Toronto, 1992.

Milne, Courtney. *The Sacred Earth.* Saskatoon, Saskatchewan: Western Producer Prairie Books, 1991. Toronto: Penguin Books, 1992.

Mystic Places. Alexandria: Time Life, 1987.

Nabokov, Peter. *Native American Testimony, A Chronicle of Indian-White Relations from Prophecy to the Present, 1492-1992.* New York: Penguin (Viking), 1992.

Natural Wonders of the World. Montreal: Reader's Digest Association Inc., 1980.

Newcomb, W. W. Jr. *The Indians of Texas, From Prehistoric to Modern Times.* Austin: University of Texas Press, 1961-1990.

Niehardt, John G. *Black Elk Speaks.* Lincoln, Nebraska: University of Nebraska Press, 1988.

Noble, David Grant. *Ancient Ruins of the Southwest.* Flagstaff, Arizona: Northland Publishing, 1981, 1991.

Nu-tka-, "Captain Cook and the Spanish Explorers on the Coast." *Sound Heritage,* Vol. VII. Number I. Victoria, British Columbia: Aural History Provincial Archives, 1978.

Nu-tka-, The History and Survival of Nootkan Culture. *Sound Heritage,* Volume VII, No. 2. Victoria, British Columbia: Aural History Provincial Archives, 1978.

Ortiz, Alfonso, ed. *Handbook of North American Indians,* Vol. 9, Southwest. Washington, DC: Smithsonian Institute, 1979.

Patterson, Alex. *A Field Guide to Rock Art Symbols of the Greater Southwest.* Boulder: Johnson Book, 1992.

Pearen, Shelley J. *Exploring Manitoulin.* Toronto: University of Toronto Press, 1992.

Pennick, Nigel. *Earth Harmony.* London: Century, 1987.

Pennick, Nigel. *Geomancy: The Ancient Science of Man in Harmony with the Earth.* London: Thames and Hudson, 1979.

People of the Desert. Alexandria: Time Life, 1993.

Peterson, Natasha. *Sacred Sites: A Traveler's Guide to North America's Most Powerful, Mystical Landmarks.* Chicago: Contemporary Books Inc., 1988.

Pike, Donald G. and David Muench. *Anasazi: Ancient People of the Rock.* New York: Harmony Books, 1974.

Place, Chuck. *Ancient Walls, Indian Ruins of the Southwest.* Golden, Colorado: Fulcrum Publishing, 1992.

Price, Joan Ellen. *Sacred Mountains: Ways of Knowledge.* Manuscript.

Ray, Dorothy Jean. *Eskimo Masks: Art and Ceremony.* University of Washington Press, 1967.

Realm of the Iroquois. Alexandria: Time Life, 1993.

Reeves, Brian O.K., and Margaret Kennedy. *Kunaitupii, Coming Together on Native Sacred Sites.* Calgary, Alberta: Archeological Society of Alberta, 1993.

Reid, Bill, and Robert Bringhurst. *The Raven Steals the Light.* Vancouver: Douglas and McIntyre, 1984.

Roberts, Elizabeth, and Elias Amidon. *Earth Prayers From Around the World.* San Francisco: HarperCollins, 1991.

Roseau River Three Fires Society. *The Creek Study, An Anishanabe Understanding of the Petroforms.* Winnipeg, Manitoba: Parks Branch, Manitoba Dept. of Natural Resources, 1990.

Ross, Dr. Allen C., and Mitakuye Oyasin. "We Are All Related." Kyle, South Dakota: Bear, 1989.

Roszak, Theodore. *The Voice of the Earth.* New York: Simon and Schuster, 1992.

Sabo, George. *Paths of Our Children.* Fayetteville, Arkansas: Arkansas Archeological Survey, 1992.

Sams, Jamie, and David Carson. *Medicine Cards: The Discovery of Power Through the Ways of Animals.* Sante Fe: Bear and Co., 1988.

Schaafsma, Polly. *Indian Rock Art of the Southwest.* Albuquerque: University of New Mexico Press, 1980.

Sherman, Josepha. *Indian Tribes of North America.* New York, Portland House, 1990.

Silko, Leslie. *Storyteller.* New York: Little Brown and Co., 1981.

Silverberg, Robert. *The Mound Builders.* Athens, Ohio: Ohio University Press, 1989.

South Dakota Writers' Project, and Oscar Howe. *Legends of the Mighty Sioux.* Interior, South Dakota: Badlands Natural History Association, 1987.

Spirit World, The. Alexandria, Virginia: Time Life, 1992.

Sproule, Barbara C. *Primal Myths: Creating the World.* New York: Harper and Row, 1979.

Steiger, Brad. *Indian Medicine Power.* Westchester, Pennsylvania: Schiffer Publishing, 1984.

Storm, Hyemeyohsts. *Seven Arrows.* New York, Ballantyne Books, 1972.

Stuart, Gene S. *America's Ancient Cities.* Washington, D.C., National Geographic Society, 1988.

Sun Bear, and Wabun. *The Medicine Wheel, Earth Astrology.* New York: Prentice Hall, 1980.

Sun Bear, Wabun Wind, and Crysalis Mulligan. *Dancing With the Wheel. The Medicine Wheel Workbook.* New York, Simon and Shuster, 1991.

Sutphen, Dick. *Sedona: Psychic Energy Vortexes.* Malibu, California: Valley of the Sun Printing Co., 1986.

Suttles, Wayne, ed. *Handbook of North American Indians,* Vol. 7, Northwest Coast. Washington, DC: Smithsonian, 1990.

Swan, James. *Sacred Places: How the Living Earth Seeks Our Friendship.* Santa Fe: Bear and Co., 1990.

Swan, James, ed. *The Power of Place and Human Environment.* Wheaton, Illinois: Quest Books, 1991.

Swinton, George. *Eskimo Sculpture.* Toronto: McClelland & Stewart, 1965.

The Sacred Tree. Lethbridge, Alberta: Four Worlds Development Press, 1984.

Trigger, Buce C., ed. *Handbook of North American Indians,* Vol. 15, Northeast. Washington, DC: Smithsonian, 1978.

Viele, Catherine W. *Voices in the Canyon.* Southwest Parks and Monuments, 1990.

Wabun, and Barry Weinstock. *Sun Bear, The Path of Power.* Spokane: Bear Tribe Publishing, 1983.

Wall, Steve, and Harvey Arden. *Wisdomkeepers, Meetings with Native American Spiritual Elders.* Hillsboro, Oregon: Beyond Words Publishing, 1990.

Waters, Frank. *Masked Gods.* Athens, Ohio: Ohio University Press, 1984.

Waters, Frank. *Book of the Hopi.* New York: Penguin (Viking), 1963, 1972–1977.

Westwood, Jennifer, ed. *The Atlas of Mysterious Places.* New York: Weidenfeld and Nicolson, 1987.

Wicklein, John. "Sprit Paths of the Anasazi," in *Archeology,* Jan./Feb. 1994, p. 36–41. New York: Archeological Institute.

Williamson, Ray. *Living the Sky: The Cosmos of the American Indian.* University of Oklahoma Press, 1984.

Wosien, Maria Gabriele. *Sacred Dance: Encounter with the Gods.* Avon, 1974.

Wright, Ronald. *Stolen Continents—The "New World" Through Indian Eyes Since 1492.* Toronto: Penguin (Viking), 1992.

Young, Dudley. *Origins of the Sacred.* New York: HarperCollins, 1991.

Zambucka, Kristin. *The Keepers of the Earth,* Honolulu: Harrane Publishing, 1985.

Zanger, Michael. *Mt. Shasta: History, Legend and Lore.* Berkeley: Celestial Arts, 1992.

Zeilinger, Ron. *Sacred Ground, Reflections on Lakota Spirituality and the Gospel.* Chamberlain, South Dakota: Tipi Press, 1987.

INDEX